30-SECOND
ANCIENT CHINA

30-SECOND
ANCIENT CHINA

The 50 most important
achievements of a timeless
civilization, each explained
in half a minute

Editor
Yijie Zhuang

Contributors
Qin Cao
Beichen Chen
Wengcheong Lam
Siran Liu
Sai Ma
Peng Peng
Chao Tang
Li Zhang
Yijie Zhuang

Illustrations
Ivan Hissey

Ivy Press

First published in Great Britain in 2015 by
Ivy Press
210 High Street, Lewes,
East Sussex BN7 2NS, U.K.
www.ivypress.co.uk

British Library Cataloguing-in-
Publication Data
A CIP catalogue record for this
book is available from the
British Library.

ISBN: 978-1-78240-270-1

This book was conceived,
designed and produced by
Ivy Press
210 High Street, Lewes,
East Sussex BN7 2NS, U.K.
www.ivypress.co.uk

Creative Director **Peter Bridgewater**
Publisher **Susan Kelly**
Editorial Director **Tom Kitch**
Art Director **Michael Whitehead**
Senior Project Editor **Caroline Earle**
Commissioning Editor **Sophie Collins**
Designer **Ginny Zeal**
Illustrator **Ivan Hissey**
Picture Researcher **Sharon Dortenzio**
Glossaries Text **Andrew Kirk**

Cover image: Shutterstock / Fotokon

Typeset in Section

Printed and bound in China

Colour origination by
Ivy Press Reprographics

10 9 8 7 6 5 4 3 2 1

Distributed worldwide (except North America) by
Thames & Hudson Ltd., 181A High Holborn,
London WC1V 7QX, United Kingdom

CONTENTS

INTRODUCTION
Yijie Zhuang

Students of ancient Chinese history and culture
face a number of distinctive questions. Why and how did China, with its
huge geographical landmass and multiple nations, remain united for
thousands of years? Why is traditional Chinese architecture so different
from that in other parts of the world? Why did a borrowed technology,
metallurgy, play such a fundamental role in ancient Chinese societies,
marking a departure from Western counterparts? Why did the population
remain high throughout history? And most importantly, when did the
concept of China, culturally and geographically, come into being?

Though fostered during Neolithic times, it was at the beginning of
the Bronze Age that many of these characteristics were shaped and
developed. Indeed, the Bronze Age, with its long timespan including the
Xia, Shang and Zhou periods (c. 4100–221 BCE), saw an acceleration in
social complexity; this was closely related to state formation, but also
created a network of economic production, state management and ritual
activities that were intertwined in a manner which came to define China.

Numerous archaeological discoveries have illuminated aspects of
ancient Chinese societies. Yet outside scholarly circles, the general public,
particularly in the West, knows very little about these civilizations. Language
has been a major barrier, but the trajectory of modern archaeological
practice has also been critical in hampering intellectual exchange.

Keeping the same framework that is adopted in other volumes of this
series, we have paid particular attention to topics that are sometimes
neglected in China and have highlighted those characteristics that are
distinctive to ancient China. Each entry is made up of a **30-second history**
which delves into the subject, further distilled into a **3-second survey**,
with an additional **3-minute excavation** raising a question or an interesting
detail which is explored further. Feature spreads in each chapter focus on
the lives and careers of some of the most intriguing figures in ancient
China. A list of further reading is provided at the end of the book for
those who want to pursue particular issues in more depth.

Great discoveries
The unique nature of ancient Chinese society and culture is gradually being uncovered through the examination of archaeological finds such as these ritual figures from Sanxingdui, though much remains to be fully explained.

Our journey begins with the **Land, Architecture & States** chapter by investigating how the long-lasting agricultural civilization in China was shaped by its unique environment, how archaeologists have tackled the perishable earth-and-wood architecture and how different state-managing strategies were employed during different periods. Complementary information is provided in **Great Discoveries**, where we choose ten of the most spectacular recent archaeological discoveries, which together represent a panorama of the Xia, Shan and Zhou cultures: cities and urban centres, rich bronze hoards and spectacular state cemeteries.

Utilizing up-to-date research on the development of metallurgy and bronze casting in China, the **Bronze & Rituals** chapter emphasizes the development of rituals, which played a central role in state management. In **Science & Society**, we offer some snapshots of daily life in the light of economic and scientific developments in the Bronze Age. As in ancient Egypt, the interment of the dead was a central focus of the living. A hierarchy in mortuary practice was established and gradually enforced more strictly, particularly among the Western Zhou people, and the prestige of the past became the purpose of the present. The constant engagement of Bronze Age people in China with their ancestors will be explored in **Afterlife & Beliefs**.

The uniqueness of Chinese writing had significant historical implications, and the early development of a continuous writing tradition is introduced in **Writing & Philosophy**. This is supplemented by a further exploration of the Warring State philosophies (a Golden Age for ancient Chinese philosophy) and the scribal tradition, another distinctive characteristic of Chinese history. The last chapter deals with **Warfare, Transportation & Trade**, in light of recent archaeological discoveries and research. As in other early states, war was an important means of obtaining social power. Although answers to some important questions remain cloudy, in this last section we aim to sketch out the expanding, interconnected network of interaction between ancient China and its neighbours in the Bronze Age.

CHRONOLOGY[1]

Xia period
c. 2100–1600 BCE

Shang period – before Anyang/Yinxu
c. 1600–1300 BCE

Shang period – Anyang/Yinxu
1300–1045 BCE
Pan Geng–Xiao Yi c. 1300–1251 BCE
Wu Ding c. 1250–1190 BCE
Zu Geng–Kang Ding c. 1190–1150 BCE
Wu Yi–Ding Xin
c. 1150–1049/1046/1043 BCE[2]

Western Zhou period
c. 1049/1046/1043–771 BC
King Wu 1049/1046/1043–1043 BCE
King Cheng 1042–1021 BCE
King Kang 1020–996 BCE
King Zhao 995–977 BCE
King Mu 976–922 BCE
King Gong 922–900 BCE
King Yih 899–892 BCE
King Xiao 891–886 BCE
King Yi 885–878 BCE
King Li 877–841 BCE
Gong He 841–828 BCE[3]
King Xuan 827–782 BCE
King You 781–771 BCE

Eastern Zhou period
770–256 BCE
Spring and Autumn period
770–476 BCE
King Ping 770–720 BCE
King Huan 719–697 BCE
King Zhuang 696–682 BCE
King Xi 681–677 BCE
King Hui 676–652 BCE
King Xiang 651–619 BCE
King Qing 618–613 BCE
King Kuang 612–607 BCE
King Ding 606–586 BCE
King Jian 585–572 BCE
King Ling 571–545 BCE
King Jing 544–520 BCE
King Jing 519–476 BCE

Warring States period
475–256 BCE
King Yuan 475–469 BCE
King Zhending 468–441 BCE
King Kao 440–426 BCE
King Wei Lie 425–402 BCE
King An 401–376 BCE
King Lie 375–369 BCE
King Xian 368–321 BCE
King Shenjing 320–315 BCE
King Nan 314–256 BCE

Qin state
777–221 BCE[4]
Duke of Xiang 777–766 BCE
Duke of Wen 765–716 BCE
Duke of Ning 715–704 BCE
Duke of Chu 703–698 BCE
Duke of Wu 697–678 BCE
Duke of De 677–676 BCE
Duke of Xuan 675–664 BCE
Duke of Cheng 663–660 BCE
Duke of Mu 659–621 BCE
Duke of Kang 620–609 BCE
Duke of Gong 608–604 BCE
Duke of Huan 603–577 BCE
Duke of Jing 576–537 BCE
Duke of Ai 536–501 BCE
Duke of Hui 500–491 BCE
Duke of Dao 490–477 BCE
Duke of Ligong 476–443 BCE
Duke of Zao 442–429 BCE
Duke of Huai 428–425 BCE
Duke of Ling 424–415 BCE
Duke of Jian 414–400 BCE
Duke of Hui 399–387 BCE
Chuzi 386–385 BCE
Duke of Xian 384–362 BCE
Duke of Xiao 361–338 BCE
King Huiwen 337–311 BCE
King Wu 310–307 BCE
King Zhao 306–251 BCE
King Xiaowen 250 BCE
King Zhuangxiang 249–247 BCE
King Zheng 246–221 BCE

Notes
1 There are numerous scholarly opinions concerning the chronology of the Xia, Shang and Zhou periods. Here we have adopted the Xia-Shang-and-Zhou periodization project, published in 2000.
2 The exact year when the last King of Shang, Ding Xin, was overthrown remains highly controversial. There are three main suggestions: 1049, 1046 or 1043 BCE.
3 841 BCE is the first point at which Chinese history has an unambiguous chronicle.
4 Qin was one of the many regional states during the Eastern Zhou period when the power of the Zhou royal court was significantly weakened. Its chronicle is partially parallel with that of the Zhou royal court, but the latter disappeared in 256 BCE while the former continued until it united China in 221 BCE under King Zheng, who became the first Emperor under the name Qinshihuangdi.

LAND, ARCHITECTURE & STATES

LAND, ARCHITECTURE & STATES
GLOSSARY

alluvium a loose aggregation of particles of soil, sand, clay or gravel which is alternately eroded and deposited by the actions of a river or other flowing body of water; alluvial soils are often highly fertile and can contain ores of precious metals such as gold and silver.

cult the ceremonial practices relating to the worship and service required by a deity or deities. This can involve specific rituals that have to be performed regularly, the erection of buildings to 'house' the deity, votive offerings of objects or goods and the sacrifice of animals or even humans. Participation in cultic practices might be limited to certain sectors of society as a means of establishing hierarchies of status, and control of the cult in the ancient world was frequently a prerequisite of political power.

feudalism a system of social organization, prevalent in medieval Europe, which involved the granting of land by a noble landowner or monarch in exchange for military support from the grantee. The person holding the land was known as the lord's vassal, and the relationship was contractually agreed through the swearing of an oath. The system extended downwards in turn to the peasants or serfs, who worked the land on behalf of their lord in return for his protection.

floodplain the region adjoining a river that is inundated when the river bursts its banks, for example during periods of heavy rainfall or as a result of snowmelt. Floodplains are characteristically fertile and form rich ecosystems, and the floodplains of rivers such as the Nile, Indus and the Yellow river were the cradles of early civilizations.

monsoon a seasonally reversing wind that carries a large amount of moisture inland during the warmer months when the land temperature rises relative to that of the sea. As this air rises the moisture precipitates to generate extended periods of rainfall. During the cooler months the cycle reverses, and a period of drought ensues.

rammed earth a building technique whereby walls are built by compacting layers of earth into an externally supported wooden frame.

Spring and Autumn period of Chinese history between 771 BCE and 475 BCE, corresponding roughly to the first part of the Eastern Zhou dynasty, when the authority of the Zhou extended over a smaller area than hitherto, and a number of smaller fiefdoms became increasingly independent. The period takes its name from the *Spring and Autumn Annals*, a chronicle of Lu state during this time which tradition attributes to Confucius.

tributary system practice whereby states wishing to trade with China were obliged to recognize Chinese superiority and pre-eminence in the region, and to send tribute 'missions' to the Chinese court. These involved the performance of particular rituals and the provision of gifts or hostages as a means of acknowledging the superior status of China.

Warring States period following on from the Spring and Autumn period, 475 BCE to 221 BCE, roughly corresponding to the second part of the Eastern Zhou dynasty. As the Zhou weakened, various smaller states struggled for supremacy, and various alliances and wars took place, culminating in the victory of Qin state and the unification of China under Emperor Qinshihuang in 221 BCE.

RIVERS & MONSOONS

the 30-second history

3-SECOND SURVEY
Although the Egyptian type of floodplain cultivation likely did not happen until the Han period, rivers fed by monsoons played a critical role in the ebb and flow of Bronze Age cultures.

3-MINUTE EXCAVATION
Although hard evidence of waterway transportation in the Bronze Age is lacking, the migration and expansion of society in central China undoubtedly benefitted from rivers. Panlong City was a Shang military outpost built right next to the Fuhe river, which connected to the Yangtze river. It is thus very likely that the Shang arrived via the rivers. Some Eastern Zhou bronze vessels have inlaid decorative motifs illustrating scenes of water battles. The boats shown were big enough to accommodate tens or hundreds of people.

The history of ancient China was profoundly shaped by its environment, a unique combination of long, sinuous rivers and short-lived but recurrent monsoons. Each summer, the East Asian and Indian summer monsoons brought copious rainfall pouring down into the rivers. But decadal cycles between disastrous floods and extreme droughts caused by abnormal monsoon activities posed a great threat to the society. This changeable water regime was so significant to farmers that, beneficial as the Yellow river has been, it has also been characterized as 'China's tribulation'. To avoid disastrous floods, the Bronze Age peoples often established their permanent settlements along small or medium-sized rivers. Erlitou, the earliest Bronze Age urban centre, was built on the terrace of the ancient Yiluo river, which undergoes active alluvial processes. Part of the site is covered by alluvial deposits or cut by recent river channels. Active alluviation, on the other hand, also promotes the formation of riverine wetlands, which offered the Erlitou people rich natural resources. By the Spring-and-Autumn and Warring States periods, large irrigation canals had been dug in north China to direct river water to farmland. But it is not until the Han period that we see the great migration of farming villages to the floodplains of the lower Yellow river, a process that had mixed results.

RELATED HISTORIES
See also
ERLITOU
page 32

FOOD
page 76

MILITARY & WEAPONS
page 138

3-SECOND BIOGRAPHY
DAYU (GREAT YU)
C. 2200–2100 BCE
Legendary founder of the Xia dynasty, a hero of the Xia tribe who tamed the floods.

30-SECOND TEXT
Yijie Zhuang

Fluctuations in the water supply meant the Bronze Age Chinese were at the mercy of floods or drought.

OWNERSHIP
OF LAND

the 30-second history

Due to the lack of contemporary written documents, no clear picture can be drawn about land ownership in early Bronze Age China. During the late Shang period, the oracle bone inscriptions unearthed at Yinxu indicate the existence of land that belonged to the Shang king, with labourers being summoned to work on the land. In the Zhou period, every square inch of the land, in theory, belonged to the Zhou king personally. The king gifted parcels of land to the Zhou elites to reward them for service or to ensure their loyalty. However, a regional ruler could also claim ownership of the land in the state that he ruled. Especially during time of war, land could be seized from a conquered state without consultation with its nominal owner. On the other hand, bronze inscriptions of the Western Zhou period indicate that land could be exchanged among elites or used as compensation, though it was not yet considered private property. From the late Western Zhou period onwards, a series of economic reforms, including reforms to land ownership, started to take place. The reforms initiated by Shang Yang in the 4th century BCE were among the most significant of these. However, whether land actually became private property as a result of these reforms is still a matter for debate.

3-SECOND SURVEY
Inscriptions on bronze wares dating to the Western Zhou period have shed light on land ownership of that time.

3-MINUTE EXCAVATION
A bronze plate with Sanshi inscriptions is one of the most significant textual documents regarding land ownership during the late Western Zhou period. It was unearthed during the reign of Emperor Qianlong (1736–95 CE) at Fengxiang, Shaanxi province. The plate has a text of 357 Chinese characters. The inscriptions on it document a land compensation made by Ze state to its neighbouring San state, where the plate was almost certainly cast. The King of Zhou is also mentioned in the inscriptions.

RELATED HISTORIES
See also
ORACLE BONE INSCRIPTIONS
page 116

BRONZE INSCRIPTIONS
page 118

3-SECOND BIOGRAPHY
SHANG YANG (LORD SHANG)
C. 390–338 BCE
Statesman in the state of Qin, whose reforms contributed greatly to the phenomenal rise of the Qin state.

30-SECOND TEXT
Li Zhang

In the Western Zhou dynasty, the Zhou king, in theory, owned every inch of the land.

POPULATION

the 30-second history

The earliest record of the population of China was drawn up around the Western Han period (206 BCE–8 CE). According to the written record, the number of households at that time amounted to 12,233,062, and the population was 59,594,978. The population before then can only be roughly estimated, based on archaeological excavations at settlements and rare records in historical documents. During the early Bronze Age, the population of the Erlitou site at its peak might have been 18,000–30,000. Based on the number and size of settlements, the total population during the early Shang period might have been around 4,000,000 to 4,500,000. The number might have risen to around 7,800,000 during the late Shang period. According to historical documents, a census was conducted during the Western Zhou period. Unfortunately, no record of the population from that time has been preserved. The population grew during the Eastern Zhou period. Based on the number of military personnel, the population during the Warring States period might have reached 20,000,000. However, none of the figures given above can be taken as anything more than an estimate of the population of Bronze Age China.

3-SECOND SURVEY
Due to the lack of contemporaneous historical documentation, estimates of the Chinese population in the Bronze Age have to be based mainly on archaeological finds and educated guesswork.

3-MINUTE EXCAVATION
Judging from archaeological discoveries and written records, the ancient city of Linzi was one of the largest and richest cities in China during the Eastern Zhou period, and was famous for being one of the most populous cities of the Warring States. The ancient city of Linzi covered an area of more than 20 sq km (7.5 square miles) in total. From the account of the traveller Su Qin, there were up to 70,000 households in Linzi during the 4th and 3rd centuries BCE.

RELATED HISTORIES
See also
ERLITOU
page 32

YINXU
page 34

30-SECOND TEXT
Li Zhang

A model of Linzi, which was thought by contemporaries to be one of the most populous cities in the Warring States.

Zhou Gong, Duke of Zhou was a powerful statesman and brother of King Wu, the founder of the Zhou dynasty. He was influential in consolidating the institutions of the Zhou dynasty.

ZHOU GONG

Zhou Gong (Duke of Zhou,

c. 1100 BCE) was the brother of the first king of
the Western dynasty, King Wu. He assisted his
father and brother in launching the war against
the Shang dynasty. He also established the
political and economic institutions of the Zhou
dynasty and fixed new standards for religion,
marriage, family, morality and other aspects
of society. '*Zhou*' was his title. He was also
honoured as '*Yuan Sheng*', the first saint
in Chinese history, with his influential
philosophy being considered the foundation
of Confucianism.

King Cheng was very young when his father,
King Wu, died. His uncle, Zhou Gong, assisted
King Cheng as regent. An armed rebellion was
staged by two other brothers of King Wu and
a son of the last king of the Shang in the east
during Zhou Gong's regency. He led an army to
suppress the rebellion and subsequently built
Chengzhou, another capital city, in order to
control the eastern territories. When King
Cheng came to adulthood, Zhou Gong handed
power back to him and retired to Chengzhou.

Zhou Gong was often called 'the king' and
issued decrees as a king according to pre-
Eastern Han (c. 100 BCE) records. But after the
Eastern Han dynasty, some historians claimed
that Zhou Gong was just a regent and had never
become king. It was considered dishonourable
for a high-ranking minister and assistant to a
king to claim the throne, according to the
moral values of that time. As a model of
Confucianism, Zhou Gong should not have
overstepped his authority. Some thought that
Zhou Gong was forced to hand over power to
his nephew and that he went east not to
counter the insurgency, but as an exile.

However, the archaeological evidence
suggests a simpler picture. Inscriptions on late
Western Zhou bronzes record that Zhou Gong
indeed had great power, but his name was
never included in the lineage of Western Zhou
kings. Newly discovered bamboo slips state
that Zhou Gong went east for three years to
suppress a rebellion, which is consistent with
the content of poems about him that circulated
for 2,000 years.

Chao Tang & Yijie Zhuang

CITIES

the 30-second history

The Bronze Age cities prior to the eastern Zhou were extremely volatile. Often driven by economic needs, control of key natural resources (ore, salt, etc.) and military expansion, these cities were situated in strategically important locations and moved after resources became exhausted. According to Sima Qian's *Records of the Grand Historian*, the Shang moved their capital at least five times, which is attested by the discovery of two early Shang cities, Zhengzhou and Yanshi. The hoards of valuable bronze vessels discovered at Zhengzhou possibly capture a moment when the Shang elites had to abandon their city under extreme circumstances. The final move to Yinxu in the reign of Pan Geng inaugurated the Shang's golden age. They first built the city on the north bank of the Huan river, but soon moved it to the south bank. Yinxu was a cult centre. Located at its core are ancestral temples, elite tombs and other ritual-related buildings. These were surrounded by bronze foundries, workshops and residential buildings. The Zhou, after their conquest of the Shang, built two capitals: western Zongzhou and eastern Chengzhou. This dual-capital system worked for almost 300 years until the eastern migration of the Zhou royal house. Cities of regional states flourished thereafter, with the focus switching from politics to economic production, opening a new era of urbanization.

RELATED HISTORIES
See also
ZHOU GONG
page 20

ERLITOU
page 32

YINXU
page 34

ZHOUYUAN
page 42

3-SECOND BIOGRAPHIES
SIMA QIAN
c. 145 or 135–86 BCE
Han period historian, author of the enduring masterpiece, *Records of the Grand Historian*.

PAN GENG
c. 1300 or 1290–1260 BCE
Legendary king of the Shang, best known for having moved the Shang capital to Yinxu.

30-SECOND TEXT
Yijie Zhuang

Cities were located to protect trade routes or natural resources, and often moved to suit changing conditions.

3-SECOND SURVEY
As a result of constant political competition and economic development, the Bronze Age cities of the Xia, Shang and Zhou dynasties experienced dramatic changes in terms of planning and functions throughout the period.

3-MINUTE EXCAVATION
Drainage became an increasing challenge to the cities. In Qufu City in Lu state in present-day Shandong province, which covered an area of 10 sq km (4 square miles), immense labour was invested in laying drainage pipes (made of stone and bricks) across the city. These pipes survived intensive ploughing in historical times. In Qin Yong City, an ancestral temple was surrounded by a rectangular-shaped stone drainage ditch called 'Sanshui'.

ARCHITECTURE

the 30-second history

The use of earth and perishable

wood, rather than stone, as the primary building material is a feature distinctive to traditional Chinese architecture. A mature rammed-earth technique was developed to construct the foundations and walls of buildings. This technology relies on enormous labour investment to pile up and compress layers of earth into an externally supported wooden frame. The Shang produced bronze construction parts and used them to connect wooden partitions in palaces. This technique was quickly adopted by the elites in other areas. A hoard discovered at Yong City in Qin state featured numbers of these bronze construction elements. The Zhou began to use hollow bricks and tiles on an impressive scale. The construction of palaces became a means to showcase the taste and status of the residents. Walls made of hollow bricks were carved with beautiful motifs and painted with murals. Roofs were built using eaves tiles and complicated wooden brackets to create an overhanging section to throw rainwater clear of the building. This feature was soon developed for purely aesthetic display, a tradition that can still be seen in the Forbidden City. Floors were made of stones and bricks to guarantee domestic hygiene. Palaces were used by the elites for meetings and as ancestral temples, while commoners lived in primitive subterranean houses.

3-SECOND SURVEY
An array of new architectural techniques were invented in the Bronze Age, driven by the need of the elites to build colossal, solemn and awe-inspiring buildings.

3-MINUTE EXCAVATION
The largest palace discovered at Erlitou is 10,000 sq m (12,000 square yards) in area, and would have required 1,000 labourers working for 200 consecutive days to build. Some archaeologists think its domestic space was undivided, while others reconstruct it as being composed of 24 rooms aligned in three parallel rows, though 'rooms' might simply mean divided space without any actual walls. Most notable are the sacrificial pits discovered in the courtyard. One has at least three human skeletons forming a circle, all of whom had suffered violent death.

RELATED HISTORIES
See also
ERLITOU
page 32

YINXU
page 34

ZHOUYUAN
page 42

YONG CITY & THE QIN STATE CEMETERY
page 46

HUMAN & ANIMAL SACRIFICES
page 108

30-SECOND TEXT
Yijie Zhuang

Ancient Chinese buildings were built with a wooden skeleton, and while carved bricks and tiles were used for decorative partition walls, the load-bearing timber frame remained the basis of Chinese architecture for millennia.

STATE MANAGEMENT & BUREAUCRACY

the 30-second history

As successful as the Shang were, they had only loose control of the different regional powers. Through the establishment of a tributary system, they distributed highly valuable bronze vessels to their allies in different regions and received resources in return. They built military outposts as far afield as the central Yangtze river, but for most of the period they were busy fighting rebellions. The situation did not change much after the Zhou's conquest of the Shang. In fact, the state became even more precarious immediately after the death of King Wu. This crisis provided an opportunity for the strong leadership of Zhou Gong, the brother of King Wu. Besides establishing two capitals to consolidate the regime and crush the rebels, he sent kinsmen and relatives of the royal Ji lineage to strategic locations to create 71 regional states. This system resembled feudalism, but differed from the medieval Europe feudo-vassalic system in that there was no intimate personal relationship between the Zhou king and the regional rulers. A state bureaucracy was also developed: under the Zhou king was the Grand Protector; the Royal Household was in charge of royal affairs, whereas supervisors of land, construction and horses, and scribes took control of state-related business. This highly organized and effective system was mimicked by regional states and set the scene for later Chinese bureaucratic development.

RELATED HISTORIES
See also
DAYANGZHOU
page 38

ZHOUYUAN
page 42

RITUAL VESSELS & THEIR DISTRIBUTION
page 60

3-SECOND SURVEY
From the tributary system to the feudal system, an effective means of state management was gradually established over time. The development of the Western Zhou state bureaucracy was influential throughout Chinese history.

3-MINUTE EXCAVATION
Located in present-day Beijing, Yan was one of the earliest states established by the Zhou. Inscriptions on the Ke lei vessel discovered in an elite tomb here document for the first time the establishment of a regional state (the tomb was probably that of its founder). The inscriptions tell how the king commanded Ke to become the ruler of Yan.

3-SECOND BIOGRAPHIES
KING WU
reigned c. 1046–1043 BCE
First king of the Zhou dynasty of ancient China.

ZHOU GONG (DUKE OF ZHOU)
fl. c. 1100 BCE
The younger brother of King Wu.

KE
c. 10th century BCE
Oldest son of Zhou Gong and first ruler of Yan state.

30-SECOND TEXT
Yijie Zhuang

The distribution of prestige goods in exchange for natural resources was the basis of state control.

GREAT DISCOVERIES

GREAT DISCOVERIES
GLOSSARY

bead-welding welding is the process of joining two pieces of metal together by heating and softening them. Forge welding was the earliest method, which involves heating the metal and then hammering the separate pieces together. A bead weld uses a filler material between the pieces of metal to create a joint, called a bead.

bronze an alloy of copper and either arsenic or tin, which produces a material that is harder and more durable than copper alone. Since ores of tin and copper rarely occur in close geographical proximity, bronze working stimulated trade between different cultures in the ancient world, so that the raw materials could be brought together. Bronze can be cast into various shapes or hammered into flat sheets from ingots.

Central Plains region on the lower reaches of the Yellow river, roughly corresponding to modern-day Henan, the southern part of Hebei, the southern part of Shanxi and the western part of Shandong provinces, regarded as the centre of the world in the Chinese Bronze Age.

dynasty a line of rulers deriving from the same family or clan. Historians usually divide Chinese history into periods that take their names from the dynasty that was in power during the period under discussion.

Eurasian steppe an extensive area of grassland stretching from what is now Ukraine eastwards to Mongolia. During the Bronze Age the steppe supported the grazing herds of nomadic tribespeople, whose mobility was based on their domestication of the horse and probably sheep, goats and cattle. Their horsemanship was a great advantage in military terms, while the mobility of these tribes was significant in disseminating language and culture over a wide area. The Great Wall of China was built in part to protect the Central Plains from attack by the Eurasian nomads.

inlay a decorative technique involving the insertion of contrasting materials into depressions in the surface of the object being decorated. Inlays are frequently precious materials such as gold, silver, turquoise or jade.

lacquer a hard, shiny decorative material used to give a glossy surface to wooden objects. In China it is derived from the poisonous resin of *Toxicodendron vernicifluum*, the Chinese lacquer tree, and Chinese lacquerware has been found that dates back to the Neolithic period.

lei a type of ritual vessel for alcohol.

loess sediment formed by the accumulation of wind-borne silt, which can form layers several hundred metres thick.

mausoleum a monumental building containing the tomb of one or more people.

proto-porcelain an early form of fired and glazed ceramic ware, but without the translucency of true porcelain. Proto-porcelain has been found dating from the Shang dynasty, around 1600 BCE.

rammed earth a building technique whereby walls are built by compacting layers of earth into an externally supported wooden frame.

ramped tomb a burial chamber which is accessed via one or more ramped causeways; the number of ramps was an indicator of status in the Chinese Bronze Age.

skew chamber type of burial chamber in which the entrance passageway or ante-chamber is at an angle to the main chamber.

slag by-product of metal smelting, the material that is left after the metal has been extracted from the ore. It has a glassy surface and was used in ancient times to make items of jewellery or glassware.

turquoise a blue-green mineral that has been prized as a gemstone for thousands of years and was one of the first gems to be mined. It is often associated with copper deposits.

ERLITOU

the 30-second history

After a test excavation in 1959 at Erlitou in present-day Henan province, the archaeologist Xu Xusheng was thrilled to discover the ruins of what he believed to be the first Shang capital, Bo, established by King Tang. He did not foresee that this discovery would initiate half a century of excavations and debate on the identity of the founder of the city. It is only recently that most Chinese archaeologists have agreed that Erlitou was most likely established and occupied by the Xia, an idea first proposed by Zou Heng that was vigorously challenged in the 1970s. Of the four occupational phases, the second reached 3 sq km (1.2 square miles). It consists of a rectangular enclosed palace area surrounded by elite tombs, a ceremonial area, a bronze foundry, a turquoise workshop and various functional areas. The whole city was divided by two roads, crisscrossing next to the northeast corner of the palace area. The roads and palaces were the most significant landmark in the city, an unprecedented phenomenon predating the similar design of the Forbidden City by four millennia. Controlling the production and consumption of luxury goods was a vital strategy for the Erlitou elite to consolidate their power. Goods such as bronze plates with turquoise inlay were distributed to areas as far away as northwest China. In return, they received exotic items, such as proto-porcelain from south China.

RELATED HISTORIES
See also
CITIES
page 22

PIECE-MOULD CASTING
page 56

POTTERY PRODUCTION
page 80

3-SECOND SURVEY
The idea of 'China' was fostered at Erlitou, a village in central China where successive excavations have revealed one of the largest and earliest urban centres in Chinese history.

3-MINUTE EXCAVATION
Next to palace No. 3 a rich elite tomb with a wooden coffin was unearthed. It contained bronzes, jade, lacquers, proto-porcelain, white ceramics, numerous other types of objects and, most amazingly, a dragon-shaped turquoise object. The consumption of these luxury goods served to display the occupant's social status, which is further strengthened by the inclusion of this turquoise object with a dragon shape, a unique design appearing only in very few special contexts.

3-SECOND BIOGRAPHIES
XUSHENG XU
1888–1976
Archaeologist and historian. Organized and directed one of the earliest excavations in China at Doujitai in 1933.

ZOU HENG
1927–2005
One of the most prominent Bronze Age archaeologists in China. First person to systematically study pottery discovered at many important Bronze Age sites.

30-SECOND TEXT
Yijie Zhuang

Erlitou is the one of earliest large-scale Bronze Age urban sites to be discovered.

YINXU

the 30-second history

The significance of Yinxu was

first established when the origin of some ancient oracle bones inscribed with the names of the Shang kings was traced to the site in the early 20th century. This metropolis of the late Shang is located in Anyang, a city in north Henan province, on the banks of the Huan river. The palace area is in the middle of the site to the south of the river. More than 80 large-scale building foundations have been found, encircled by a deep moat connecting to the river. These buildings might have been used for ancestor worship, for hosting political activities by the royal families or as living quarters. Millions of oracle bones have been found on the site, offering a key to the understanding of the divination activities that once took place here. Dozens of other residential areas were scattered around the palace area, with many handicraft workshops among them. Across the Huan river to the north, 13 ramped tombs were found in the royal cemetery along with more than 2,500 sacrificial pits in the eastern section. Most of the sacrifice pits were filled with human skeletons. Although the royal tombs had been badly looted, many fine artefacts were discovered, like the 'Mother Wu' Ding-quadripod, the largest bronze artefact ever discovered from Bronze Age China.

3-SECOND SURVEY
The authenticity of early Chinese documented history was confirmed by the discovery of Yinxu, the last capital of the Shang dynasty, which was one of the earliest excavation sites in the history of Chinese archaeology.

3-MINUTE EXCAVATION
Two recently excavated workshops give an insight into craft production in Yinxu. In the Xiaomintun bronze foundry, thousands of pieces of mould debris and slag, together with bronze-casting areas, mould preparing and drying pits, give us an idea of how piece-mould casting worked. Tiesanlu was a huge bone-working workshop. Cattle, pig and deer bones were made into pins, awls and arrowheads. The remains provide us with information about the technology as well as the organization of production.

30-SECOND TEXT
Sai Ma

At almost a tonne in weight, the 'Mother Wu' quadripod is the largest Bronze Age artefact discovered in China.

SANXINGDUI

the 30-second history

Over 1,700 bronze, gold and jade artefacts and many ivory tusks were uncovered from two rectangular vertical pits in Guanghan, Sichuan province, in southwestern China in 1986. Following years of subsequent excavations, archaeologists have unveiled a walled city with large building foundations, tombs and pottery kilns. Considered one of the most significant archaeological discoveries of the 20th century in China, the Sanxingdui site has revealed glimpses of a unique Bronze Age civilization that had lain forgotten for over 3,000 years. The majority of the bronze objects recovered from the two pits remain mysterious in terms of their design and function. Sculpture forms the main category of bronzes and some gigantic masks (one 66 cm [26 in.] tall and 138 cm [54 in.] wide) are obviously too large to wear. Indeed, no parallel for them is known anywhere else in China. Furthermore, the large quantities of jade were mainly in the form of discs and blades of various designs, not the ornaments that are abundant at Yinxu. More surprisingly, most of the objects had been deliberately damaged and burned before being carefully placed layer by layer in the pits. Unfortunately, no written evidence has been found at Sanxingdui and our understanding of the site is rather limited. Viewed in conjunction with the ash and bones of animals in the pits, the objects were possibly ritual sacrificial offerings.

3-SECOND SURVEY
The Sanxingdui site is located thousands of miles away from the Central Plains, the traditional dynastic centre, and its peak is contemporary with the late Shang at Yinxu, c. 1200 BCE.

3-MINUTE EXCAVATION
The village of Sanxingdui, which literally means 'three star mounds', is named after its earthen landscape features, which are the remains of artificial rammed earth walls. This particular construction method suggests Sanxingdui's contact with Erlitou or Zhengzhou, together with some similarities in ceramics and jade blades found there. However, many of the mysteries of Sanxingdui remain to be unlocked.

RELATED HISTORIES
See also
YINXU
page 34

RITUAL VESSELS & THEIR DISTRIBUTION
page 60

30-SECOND TEXT
Qin Cao

The function of the enormous masks and sculptures discovered in deep pits at Sanxingdui remains a mystery.

DAYANGZHOU

the 30-second history

Local farmers ploughing their
fields in 1989 uncovered this Early Bronze Age
(Shang period) tomb, surpassed in richness only
by the tomb of the famous Lady Fu Hao at
Yinxu. The area where the occupant must have
been placed was covered with jade ornaments.
He was likely a military leader, as suggested by
the 232 bronze weapons unearthed. Some
bronze arrowheads, often preserved as complete
sets, were still partially covered by lacquer and
leather pieces. At the time of his death, this
warrior had at hand a huge range of vessels of
various types and from diverse sources. These
were probably inherited from his ancestors who
would have received bronze vessels from the
Shang court and other regional powers. He also
had more than 700 luxurious jade ornaments and
precious jewels. The local contribution to this
rich inventory was over 100 items of high-
temperature hard ceramics and proto-porcelains.
Some were decorated with distinctive geometric
motifs of local styles; others had carved symbols
on the surface, possibly the name of the potter.
How did the occupant become so rich? This
region has many copper-mining sites that were in
use for thousands of years. The occupant and his
group controlled and exported this resource,
receiving valuable goods in return. The region's
own luxury items, proto-porcelain, appeared in
central China as early as the Erlitou period.

3-SECOND SURVEY
Located in a strategically
important position near
the Yangtze river, the
occupant of this tomb
enjoyed long-term
trading relationships
with the Shang and
other regional powers.

3-MINUTE EXCAVATION
Situated on the floodplain
of the Ganjiang river, a
major tributary of the
Yangtze river, the survival
of the Dayangzhou tomb
from erosion is a pure
miracle. Because of the
sandy deposits into which
it was dug, archaeologists
could hardly recognize the
shape of the chamber.
They failed to identify
traces of a complete
coffin, apart from some
pieces of decayed wood
and organic materials.

RELATED HISTORIES
See also
STATE MANAGEMENT
& BUREAUCRACY
page 26

YINXU
page 34

POTTERY PRODUCTION
page 80

30-SECOND TEXT
Yijie Zhuang

*The bronze and jade
objects in the tomb
are testament to the
power and status of
those who controlled
the region's natural
resources.*

Li Ji is considered the 'Father of Chinese Archaeology' and discovered the ancient Shang capital at Anyang. His systematic approach to the study of archaeology has been influential throughout China.

LI JI

Li Ji (1896–1979), regarded as the 'Father of Chinese Archaeology', is one of the most important anthropologists and archaeologists in 20th-century China. In 1918, as a graduate of the Tsinghua College, he joined the Boxer Indemnity Scholarship Program to study in the United States, and gained China's first doctorate in anthropology at Harvard University in 1923. After a short stay at Nankai University, Li came back to Tsinghua and joined the newly established Academy of Chinese Learning in 1925. He started his career in archaeology by leading the Xiyincun excavation in 1926, the very first archaeological excavation carried out by Chinese scholars. Xiyincun's success, as well as his dedication to fieldwork, led to Li later becoming director of the Division of Archaeology of the Academia Sinica, and also led him to 'the cause of his life' – Anyang.

As the Shang capital before the first millennium BCE, Anyang remained unknown to the world until the late 1920s, when Li and his team excavated the Shang palace, and found archaeological evidence of oracle bones, ritual bronzes, pottery and so on. In 1937, the outbreak of war forced Li to stop the fieldwork, and escort all the archaeological records from one place to another, and eventually to Taiwan in 1948.

Afterwards, as the founder of the Department of Anthropology at the National Taiwan University, and the head of the Institute of History and Philology, Li dedicated the last 30 years of his life to the study of Anyang materials. Using scientific approaches, he standardized terminology, and introduced typology into his archaeological work. He also devoted himself to co-operating with museums, protecting archaeological resources and providing a training ground for new generations of archaeologists.

Li Ji's final book, *Anyang*, published in 1977, is a portrait of his life of archaeology.

Beichen Chen & Chao Tang

ZHOUYUAN

the 30-second history

In the hope of exploring the capitals of the Zhou dynasty and guided by ancient texts, the archaeologist Chang-ju Shih investigated Zhouyuan for the first time in the 1940s. Over the following decades, bronze hoards, tombs, building foundations and workshops were discovered, and the site came to be regarded as the pre-dynastic capital from which the Zhou people later conquered the Shang. It is a huge site with a maximum area of 30 sq km (11.5 square miles). Reservoirs and water channels, together with natural gullies and man-made wells, give us a picture of its water supply system. Large building foundations have been found, usually made of rammed earth. These are believed to be either palaces or the ancestral temples of the elites. Thousands of inscribed turtle shell fragments were unearthed in foundations near the modern village of Fengchu. The characters carved on them are so small that they could be regarded as miniatures. Bronze foundries, Jue-earring workshops and bone workshops indicate a high degree of standardization and specialization, demonstrating Zhouyuan's status as an economic centre. However, its role as the pre-dynastic capital has been challenged, mainly because of the lack of prestige remains and goods from the proto-Zhou period. Zhouyuan is certainly important, but its historical position needs further exploration.

3-SECOND SURVEY
Located on the south margin of the loess plateau area in northwest China, Zhouyuan, the 'Plain of Zhou', is one of the most important capitals of the proto-Zhou period and a capital-like city of the Western Zhou dynasty.

3-MINUTE EXCAVATION
In ancient texts, Zhouyuan was described as fertile land where bitter edible plants like *Viola verecunda* magically became sweet. Danfu, one of the Zhou ancestors, led his clansmen there, after which the Zhou conquered the Shang. After the establishment of the Zhou dynasty, Zhouyuan was given to Zhou Gong as his fiefdom. Zhouyuan remained prosperous throughout the Western Zhou dynasty, but after the attack of the Quanrong barbarians, the survivors moved to the east and the city quickly collapsed.

RELATED HISTORIES
See also
CITIES
page 22

ARCHITECTURE
page 24

PIECE-MOULD CASTING
page 56

DIVINATION & SHAMANISM
page 104

3-SECOND BIOGRAPHIES
KING WU
reigned c. 1046–1043 BCE
First king of the Zhou dynasty.

ZHOU GONG (DUKE OF ZHOU)
fl. c. 1100 BCE
The younger brother of King Wu.

CHANG-JU SHIH
1902–2004
Archaeologist and historian. A pioneer of early archaeology.

30-SECOND TEXT
Sai Ma

An inscription on this vessel describes a previous Shang family surrendered to Zhou people and settled down at Zhouyuan.

SUIZHOU ZENG MARQUIS CEMETERY

the 30-second history

RELATED HISTORIES
See also
ZHOUYUAN
page 42

STATE CEMETERIES
OF THE ZHOU
page 100

3-SECOND SURVEY
At least two generations of state rulers were buried in the Zeng Marquis cemetery, and one of their tombs is by far the largest found in the archaeology of the Western Zhou.

3-MINUTE EXCAVATION
Like other ruling classes in the Zhou period, the most powerful occupants at Yejiashan cemetery arranged their tombs on the high visibility mound, surrounded by middle-sized and smaller burials. The locations of all the important burials were carefully arranged, starting in the north with the tomb of a possible ruler, and then going south in orderly pairs of later generations. Each one has a possible ruler and his consort(s) side by side.

30-SECOND TEXT
Beichen Chen

From 2011 to 2013, two seasons of excavation at Yejiashan near the present-day city of Suizhou, north Hubei province, revealed the site of a large-scale Western Zhou state cemetery with 147 burials. Over 2,000 grave goods were uncovered, ranging from bronzes and ceramics to lacquer, jade and stoneware, reflecting a wealthy community that flourished here 3,000 years ago. This collection of luxury artefacts derives from multiple disparate sources. Some ideas were borrowed from provincial traditions from hundreds of miles away, such as a flamboyant *lei* vessel from southwestern China, and the tiger-shaped flanges on a bell from further south. The majority of the bronzes indicated that the ancient Hubei people had adopted a very similar ritual sequence to the Zhou metropolitan areas in the north. Some of them were inscribed with ancient Chinese characters, for example, 'Marquis of Zeng', implying that the owner saw himself as the ruler of a Zhou regional power, the state of Zeng. Although ignored in most of the historical texts known to us, previous discoveries indicated that the Zeng controlled the area from the end of the 9th century to the mid-4th century BCE. By pushing back this timeline another 200 years, the newly excavated Yejiashan makes the Zeng one of the longest-lived regional powers in the whole Zhou period.

The range of goods indicates that this community was widely connected with other Bronze Age regions.

YONG CITY & THE QIN STATE CEMETERY

the 30-second history

Following clues from ancient texts, archaeologists had begun to look for the legendary Yong City in the 1930s, and at Fengxiang county in Shaanxi province a site covering 51 sq km (19.5 square miles) was discovered. Within the city is a palace district, workshops, a marketplace and residential areas for commoners. One of the large foundations found near the modern village of Majiazhuang comprises a rectangular wall with one big building located in the middle and two small ones to the south. Its layout is exactly the same as the descriptions from ancient texts of an ancestral shrine. Hundreds of sacrificial pits in the middle yard confirm this assumption. Yong City was so important in the history of the Qin that important ceremonies, like the coronation of Emperor Qinshihuang, were held there even after the capital had been moved elsewhere. Fourteen huge mausoleums were located in the southwest suburb of the city. Triple trenches respectively encircle the mausoleum area, each mausoleum (some include two or more tombs) and some of the tombs. Qin tombs have always been noted for their scale. Of these, Qin Duke Tomb No. 1 is the largest ever to have been excavated in China. It is 300 m (328 yards) long and 24 m (26 yards) deep, with 186 human sacrifices, and is believed to be the tomb of Duke Jing.

3-SECOND SURVEY
Yong City was the capital city of Qin for nearly 300 years from 677 to 383 BCE, which made it the most enduring capital city in the history of Qin state.

3-MINUTE EXCAVATION
The layout of the cemetery could be regarded as a transitional form between the previous 'centralized royal cemetery system' and the subsequent 'independent mausoleum system'. In the Shang and Western Zhou periods, multiple generations of state rulers were buried in the same cemetery, with their own tomb but without an independent mausoleum. However, from the period of Yong City, the independent mausoleum system became much more popular, and later on, in the Qin and Han dynasties, it was fully established.

RELATED HISTORIES
See also
CITIES
page 22

ARCHITECTURE
page 24

HUMAN & ANIMAL SACRIFICES
page 108

3-SECOND BIOGRAPHIES
DUKE JING OF QIN
reigned 576–537 BCE
The 18th ruler of Qin state.

EMPEROR QINSHIHUANG
reigned 246–221 BCE
as king of Qin state
reigned 221–210 BCE
as emperor of Qin dynasty
He conquered all the other warring states, united China, established the Qin dynasty and became the first emperor in Chinese history.

30-SECOND TEXT
Sai Ma

This model shows the tomb of Duke Jing, one of the most significant finds at the ancient Qin capital city.

MAJIAYUAN

the 30-second history

Since the crackdown on tomb robbery at Majiayuan in northwest China in 2006, archaeological work has uncovered more than 20 tombs of the late Warring States period from the total of 59 tombs and sacrificial pits in the cemetery. The structure of the tombs is extremely unusual compared with those found previously in this area. Most of the tombs have a vertical earth-pit with a skew chamber and a stepped tomb tunnel. The steps are usually made up of odd numbers like 9, 7, 5, 3 and 1, which probably represents a social hierarchy. Animal sacrifices were popular, as indicated by the large number of horse, cattle and sheep skulls and forelegs found. Objects unearthed from the tombs show multicultural factors. The tiger-shaped and bighorn sheep-shaped ornaments on the chariots may be influenced by the Eurasian steppe culture, while the widespread use of gold and silver, the appearance of glass and gold bead-welding technology could be related to western cultures, such as the Mediterranean, Pazyryk and Scythian. The cocoon-shaped *Hu*-jar is a typical Qin cultural object and the spade-shaped foot *Li*-tripod derives from the indigenous Xirong culture. It is obvious that the Xirong culture played a very important role in cultural exchange between the west and the east.

3-SECOND SURVEY
Majiayuan is a recently excavated cemetery in Gansu province in northwest China, which is believed to be the cemetery of the so-called Xirong (barbarians in the west) tribe.

3-MINUTE EXCAVATION
Among the remarkable discoveries at Majiayuan cemetery are the luxurious chariots in the tomb tunnel and the chamber. Most of the chariots are decorated with lacquer and glittering bronze, silver and gold ornaments, usually of hollow geometric and animal motifs. These decorations are found on nearly all parts of the chariots. They are so over-decorated that scholars believe they were meant only for ritual and funeral purposes rather than everyday use.

30-SECOND TEXT
Sai Ma

The artefacts discovered in the tombs at Majiayuan are suggestive of ancient Eurasian steppe cultures and indicate that the owner of the tomb might be one of the so-called 'barbarians in the west'.

BRONZES & RITUALS

BRONZES & RITUALS
GLOSSARY

bronze an alloy of copper and either arsenic or tin, which produces a material that is harder and more durable than copper alone. Since ores of tin and copper rarely occur together, bronze working stimulated trade between different cultures in the ancient world. Bronze can be cast into various shapes or hammered into flat sheets from ingots.

Central Plains region on the lower reaches of the Yellow river, roughly corresponding to modern-day Henan, the southern part of Hebei, the southern part of Shanxi and the western part of Shandong provinces, regarded as the centre of the world in the Chinese Bronze Age.

inlay a decorative technique involving the insertion of contrasting materials into depressions in the surface of the object being decorated. Inlays are frequently made with precious materials such as gold, silver, turquoise or jade.

ocarina a type of vessel wind instrument, often ovoid and made of ceramic material or bone, with a mouthpiece and holes to vary the pitch of the note.

radiocarbon dating method of establishing the age of an organic object by measuring the level of radiocarbon, a radioactive isotope of carbon, remaining in it. Living organisms exchange carbon with the biosphere, and so have the same level of radiocarbon as the surrounding environment. Once they are dead this exchange ceases, and the radiocarbon starts to decay. Since radiocarbon decays at a known rate, comparing the amount of radiocarbon in an object with the amount in the environment will give an estimate of when the organism died.

ritual a sequence of activities usually carried out in a religious context, which may involve specific words or actions, and is usually characterized by invariance, fixed forms and deference to tradition. In the Chinese Bronze Age central control of ritual was a means of maintaining the power and status of elites. The use of bronze vessels of different types characterized ritual in Bronze Age China. The evolution of such ritual vessels over time offers one method of interpreting and periodizing social and cultural changes.

smelting the process of extracting a metal from its ore. In ancient times this was achieved by heating the ore with charcoal in a kiln or furnace, the charcoal producing carbon monoxide which acts as a reducing agent, liberating the pure metal from its compound.

sumptuary laws set of regulations that control the consumption of especially luxury goods, usually by stipulating that particular foods, clothes or materials could only be used by higher social classes. Sumptuary laws were instituted as a means of establishing and maintaining social hierarchies.

welding the process of joining two pieces of metal together by heating and softening them. Forge welding was the earliest method, which involves heating the metal and then hammering the separate pieces together. A bead weld uses a filler material between the pieces of metal to create a joint, called a bead.

COPPER PRODUCTION

the 30-second history

The Chinese Bronze Age is represented by an enormous number of copper-based objects from a wide range of locations. Although the delicate decoration of these objects has often been remarked upon, little is known about where and how the metal used to manufacture them was produced. The production of metals was a serious issue, since the power of a state was largely legitimated by its control of metal-production centres. Jurisdiction over these metal sources could cause warfare between neighbouring areas, the moving of capital cities and ultimately the prosperity or decline of regional powers. Copper production involves a series of complex activities from mining to smelting, consumes considerable amounts of resources and requires a high level of labour organization. Ancient copper-production sites were usually located close to copper ore deposits and to woodland, in order to avoid the necessity of transporting heavy ores and bulky charcoal. However, it is notable that the Central Plains, the location for the most conspicuous Bronze Age cultures, has no significant copper ore deposits. This implies that the large-scale metal-casting workshops of these cultures had to import metals from other areas. Archaeologists have struggled to identify the copper sources of the cultures for the Central Plains, but still have no conclusive answer.

3-SECOND SURVEY
Copper production was vital for the ancient Chinese dynasties. The cultures in the Central Plains, although the largest consumers of copper, had no resources to produce it, and the location of their copper source is still a matter for debate.

3-MINUTE EXCAVATION
The most impressive ancient copper-production site was found in Tonglushan, in Hubei province. The excavations revealed mining galleries, ore-dressing facilities, smelting furnaces and huge heaps of slag. Significant disturbance from later mining activities means evidence is hard to date accurately. Radiocarbon dating suggests that the site might have been used in the late Shang dynasty while most of the remains were dated to the Western and Eastern Zhou periods.

RELATED HISTORIES
See also
ERLITOU
page 32

YINXU
page 34

PIECE-MOULD CASTING
page 56

RITUAL VESSELS & THEIR DISTRIBUTION
page 60

LONG-DISTANCE TRADE
page 146

30-SECOND TEXT
Siran Liu

The middle Yangtze river valley has been suggested as a source of the copper ore used in the Central Plains.

PIECE-MOULD CASTING

the 30-second history

3-SECOND SURVEY

Piece-mould casting is the hallmark of the Chinese Bronze Age cultures of the Central Plains, and played a significant role in their ritual systems.

3-MINUTE EXCAVATION

The Erlitou culture (1900–1500 BCE) has been identified as the first culture to widely adopt piece-mould casting, but some sporadic finds such as the copper 'bell' discovered at the site of Taosi (2600–2000 BCE) suggest that the roots of this technology might be in the late Neolithic period. Other issues concerning this technology such as pattern-making techniques and its relationship with lost wax casting attract abundant ongoing academic exchanges.

The most impressive technological innovation in the Chinese Bronze Age was piece-mould casting, which was employed in the large-scale production of bronze ritual vessels, musical instruments, decorative items and other artefacts. This technology characterized three Chinese Bronze Age cultures, the Erlitou, Shang and Zhou, and distinguished them from their northern and northwestern neighbours. In contrast to lost wax casting, a typical mould for piece-mould casting consists of at least three sections assembled around a core. The sectioning enables the mould to copy complex shapes and intricate patterns from a model. The gap between mould and core was filled with liquid bronze to form the artefact. The invention of piece-mould casting in the Central Plains was brought about by the institutional use of ritual vessels in China, which in itself is a cultural practice rarely identified outside of China. This industry culminated in the late Shang to early Western Zhou period when vessels became huge in size and were finely decorated with high-relief patterns. The collapse of centralized power in the late Western Zhou period had a significant impact on this industry. During the subsequent Eastern Zhou period, the sophisticated way of dividing mould sections was simplified and standardized, and cast-on, welding and inlay techniques were widely adopted.

RELATED HISTORIES

See also

ERLITOU
page 32

YINXU
page 34

LOST WAX CASTING
page 58

RITUAL REFORM &
RESTRUCTURING
page 70

30-SECOND TEXT

Siran Liu

This owl-shaped wine jar shows the capacity of piece-mould casting to reproduce intricate shapes and patterns.

LOST WAX CASTING

the 30-second history

Lost wax casting is likely the most controversial technology of the Chinese Bronze Age. Whereas some scholars claim that this technology was fully mastered by Chinese people by the Eastern Zhou period, others hold the opposite opinion, that lost wax casting never appeared in China during the Bronze Age. In contrast to piece-mould casting, lost wax casting is generally accepted as an exotic technology which was mainly used in China to manufacture elaborate decorations on bronze artefacts, rather than for figurines as in Mesopotamia and Egypt. Early evidence of this technology, though still debatable, has mostly been identified in the Chu area and its adjacent regions in central-south China during the middle Eastern Zhou period. In brief, lost wax casting technology involves creating a model of wax and covering it with clay material to form a mould around it. The mould is fired, and the molten wax drains, leaving a gap inside the mould that will be filled by the metal. Compared to the piece-mould method, lost wax casting is much more versatile in shaping any form and enables the craftsman to create considerably more sophisticated decorations on bronze artefacts, such as, for example, the renowned *Zun* vessel and *Pan* plate from the tomb of Marquis Yi of Zeng state.

RELATED HISTORIES
See also
SUIZHOU ZENG
MARQUIS CEMETERY
page 44

PIECE-MOULD CASTING
page 56

30-SECOND TEXT
Siran Liu

3-SECOND SURVEY
Lost wax casting was employed as a supplementary technology to piece-mould casting during the Chinese Bronze Age to create intricate decorations on bronze artefacts.

3-MINUTE EXCAVATION
The famous *Zun* vessel and *Pan* plate found in the tomb of Marquis Yi were decorated with a rim of intricate hollowed intertwined patterns, which was immediately recognized as evidence of lost wax casting. Nevertheless, in 2006 a group of scholars published a paper suggesting that these decorations were manufactured by means of piece-mould casting, and questioned the existence of the lost wax casting technique during the entire Chinese Bronze Age.

A clay mould used for lost-wax casting, together with the resulting decorated bronze mirror.

RITUAL VESSELS & THEIR DISTRIBUTION

the 30-second history

Bronze ritual vessels were among the most valuable products of the Shang and Western Zhou periods. Normally in the form of alcohol or food containers, ritual vessels appeared at ceremonial banquets (sometimes called sacrifices), in which they were possibly used as offerings to honour gods or family ancestors. Ritual bronzes were usually decorated with attractive motifs, and some of them were inscribed with the name of the vessel's owner and descriptions of their honours or achievements. These early writings were likely intended for gods or ancestors to read, or considering the vessel owners themselves as future ancestors, for their descendants to treasure. Originating in the Central Plains, the use of bronze ritual vessels was widespread in the metropolitan areas of the north Yellow river valley and the south Yangtze river region, covering most of the area between the two river regions and beyond. However, in some remote regions (such as Sanxingdui in Sichuan), although similar bronze vessels were involved in ritual assemblage, it is believed that the local people understood and used such ritual vessels in ways different to those of the central areas, especially the ritual performances that related to ancestor worship.

3-SECOND SURVEY
The use and significance of bronze ritual vessels related to the beliefs of ancient Chinese people and their attitude towards life and the afterlife.

3-MINUTE EXCAVATION
In field archaeology, ritual bronzes are normally found in tombs and hoards. The former constitutes the majority, where bronzes were intentionally buried so that the tomb occupant would be able to continue to offer ceremonial banquets to his or her ancestors in the afterlife. Hoards, on the other hand, are more uncommon. The largest finds in Zhouyuan, for instance, are believed to have been hastily buried when the Zhou people had to flee their homeland in the face of invaders from the west.

RELATED HISTORIES
See also
SANXINGDUI
page 36

ZHOUYUAN
page 42

DECORATION &
SOCIAL MEANINGS
page 68

30-SECOND TEXT
Beichen Chen

These bronze ritual vessels date from the Western Zhou period, the later vessel on the right shows the change to a more simple geometric palette.

THE SHAN FAMILY

On 19 January 2003, 27 bronze vessels were discovered at Yangjiacun village, Shaanxi province. They belonged to a noble family of the Western Zhou, the Shan. Inscriptions on the vessels describe a family tree from 3,000 years ago. The owner of the bronzes was Lai, who was an administrator of natural resources for King Xuan (827–782 BCE), a position that he had inherited from his ancestors. Lai also served with distinction in the war against the Xianyun, a minority tribe. He was put in charge of the captives from the war. Most of the bronzes were made after this appointment. Lai proudly listed the ranks and achievements of his ancestors on the bronzes.

The Shan family reared eight generations in the Western Zhou period, and served 12 Zhou kings. The first ancestor named was Shan Gong (Duke Shan). He assisted King Wen and King Wu in their conquest of the Shang dynasty. The second ancestor was Gong Shu, who assisted King Cheng (r. 1042–1021 BCE) to govern the regional states. The third ancestor, Xin Shi Zhong, was a minister during King Kang's reign (r. 1020–996 BCE). The fourth ancestor, Hui Zhong Li Fu, participated in the war to suppress the Chu state rebels. The fifth ancestor, Ling Bo, was an officer of King Gong and King Yi (r. 922–892 BCE). The sixth generation was Lai's grandfather, who served King Xiao and King Yi (r. 891–878 BCE). Lai's father, Gong Shu, was the seventh generation, an officer of King Li (r. 877–828 BCE). All these ancestors were virtuous men and were trusted and rewarded by the Zhou kings, serving the Zhou dynasty as officers for generations.

The Shan family was not the most powerful family of the Western Zhou dynasty, and no record of this family appears in historical texts. However, it is rare to find such a long, clear and complete family lineage inscribed on bronzes. Lai would never have anticipated that the real glory of the Shan family would come 3,000 years after he buried his bronzes.

Chao Tang & Yijie Zhuang

The Lai Pan inscriptions record the achievements of eight generations of the Shan family who served 12 kings during the Western Zhou dynasty.

MATCHING SETS OF RITUAL VESSELS

the 30-second history

The institution of matching sets

of food vessels (*ding* and *gui*) was one of the most representative developments introduced by the Ritual Reform around the mid-9th century BCE. Replacing the previous alcohol-focused vessels in various sizes and decorative styles, identical food vessels – for example, odd numbers of *ding* tripods in decreasing sizes and even numbers of *gui* vessels of the same size – formed the core equipment for sacrifices. The conversion from offering alcohol to offering food changed specific tasks in ritual performance, requiring different procedures executed by different specialists. The presence of vessels of the same shape and decoration shifted the audience's attention from individual vessels to the complete sets, which were of symbolic significance in the vessel owners' social status. According to the 'sumptuary rules' in the texts, the number of matching vessels in a set was supposed to be strictly correlated with the rank of their owner. For example, a king was entitled to nine *ding* and eight *gui*, while a minister could have five *ding* and four *gui*. Field archaeology, however, has rarely established such a one-to-one correlation. It is possible that the greater quantity sets or larger-sized vessels were made for elites with higher social status or a closer relationship to the Zhou authority, but their specific ranks are hard to discern from their vessel sets.

3-SECOND SURVEY
A move away from individual artefacts to matched sets of bronze vessels characterized the ritual practice of the mid-9th century.

3-MINUTE EXCAVATION
The idea of matching sets was probably inspired by early Western Zhou practice in Shaanxi province. One of the earliest examples, the tomb of a consort of the ruler of Yu state, revealed a simplified set of five *ding* and four *gui*, in which the vessels were identical in shape but barely decorated.

RELATED HISTORIES
See also
ZHOUYUAN
page 42

RITUAL VESSELS & THEIR DISTRIBUTION
page 60

RITUAL REFORM & RESTRUCTURING
page 70

STATE CEMETERIES OF THE ZHOU
page 100

30-SECOND TEXT
Beichen Chen

Identical ding vessels in decreasing size form one of the most important components of the matching set.

MUSICAL INSTRUMENTS

the 30-second history

3-SECOND SURVEY
Music making has a venerable history in China, and the advent of bronze technology allowed more sophisticated chiming instruments to be created.

3-MINUTE EXCAVATION
One of the most spectacular discoveries of musical instruments of the Bronze Age was from the tomb of Marquis Yi of Zeng. This tomb, dating to the 5th century BCE, is located at Leigudun, near the city of Suizhou, Hubei province, in central China. Over one hundred musical instruments were unearthed from the tomb including sixty-five bronze bells, thirty-two chime stones, seven large zithers (se), three mouth-organs (sheng), two panpipes (paixiao), two transverse flutes (di) and three drums.

Archaeological discoveries of well-preserved instruments have demonstrated a very long tradition of music making in China. Tonally precise flutes, stone chimes (qing), ovoid clay ocarinas (xun) and drums had already made their appearance prior to the Bronze Age. During the Chinese Bronze Age, more musical instruments were invented and used. With the advent of bronze casting, the first small metal bells were cast in the first half of the second millennium BCE. Chimed sets of bronze bells in a larger size (nao) started to be used by the late Shang elites (c. 1250–1050 BCE). During the Zhou dynasty, dual-toned bronze bells in sets became very significant and played an important role in rituals. Bronze bells, together with other musical instruments, provided the musical accompaniment to dances and singing in the ancestral cult. The bronze bells were suspended on wooden racks. Performers used mallets to hit the striking point for the A- or B-tone on the bells. Important evidence for the musical culture of the period was obtained from the tomb of Marquis Yi of Zeng, which contained numerous bronze bells. Uniquely, inscriptions recording the tones were cast on the bells, showing that each bell was designed to produce two tones. This discovery fundamentally changed our understanding of music during this period.

RELATED HISTORIES
See also
SUIZHOU ZENG MARQUIS CEMETERY
page 44

RITUAL VESSELS & THEIR DISTRIBUTION
page 60

3-SECOND BIOGRAPHY
MARQUIS YI OF ZENG
died c. 433 BCE
Ruler of the Zeng state, Warring States period.

30-SECOND TEXT
Li Zhang

Bronze bells were significant musical instruments during the Bronze Age of China.

DECORATION & SOCIAL MEANINGS

the 30-second history

Variations of animal-masks (known in Chinese as *taotie*), images of creatures (including both imaginary and realistic animals) and geometric motifs formed the repertoire of the ancient decorating system on Chinese bronzes. Despite time and regional differences, the principal ways of combining them were remarkably stable: the eye-based animal-mask (sometimes with winding horns and shrinking body) occupies the visual centre of the vessel, surrounded by one or more layers of subordinate patterns, such as dragons, birds and repeated geometric patterns. Before being overwhelmingly replaced in the 9th century BCE, such *taotie* and animal images had been valued by the Shang and Western Zhou ruling class for over five centuries. They are normally interpreted in terms of animal/ancestor worship, especially for religious or ceremonial occasions. Through them, ancient people believed they would have the power to communicate with their ancestors or gods. Hence, certain motifs were likely to be given symbolic meanings. For example, *taotie* could represent 'power' or 'protection'; dragons could stand for 'death'; and cicadas could mean 'rebirth'. Although the original significance of these bronze decorations has been lost in history, the mystery of their meaning paradoxically renders the visual impact of this decoration more compelling for us.

3-SECOND SURVEY
The decorative schemes of Chinese bronzes reflected the belief systems of those who commissioned these vessels.

3-MINUTE EXCAVATION
Like inscriptions, in field archaeology decoration is another 'age indicator'. Based on traditional mould-casting techniques, the animal-mask developed from a plain and undecorated design to incorporate dense intricate patterns, until the 9th century BCE when it was suddenly replaced by bands of geometric patterns. From the 6th century onwards, new casting technologies such as 'pattern-block' and 'lost wax' allowed the adoption of more complicated designs of bronze decoration.

RELATED HISTORIES
See also
PIECE-MOULD CASTING
page 56

LOST WAX CASTING
page 58

RITUAL VESSELS & THEIR DISTRIBUTION
page 60

RITUAL REFORM & RESTRUCTURING
page 70

30-SECOND TEXT
Beichen Chen

As one of the most popular motifs on bronzes, animal masks had occupied the visual centre of bronze vessels for centuries.

RITUAL REFORM & RESTRUCTURING

the 30-second history

The late Western Zhou faced a series of crises. Some of these originated from within the state, as a consequence of the expanding bureaucracy and increasing conflict among the aristocrats for land and economic resources. This necessitated a top-down reform of ritual, located at the centre of aristocratic life and involving the use of bronze vessels. Motifs and the decoration of ritual vessels changed from animal shapes and high-relief patterns to an abstract and geometric palette. Wine vessels such as jue almost disappeared from the bronze sets, and the more important role subsequently played by food vessels is evident. Several new types were added to the list of prestigious ritual vessels, but these were simple and humble forms derived from ceramic kitchen vessels. The rationale behind this reform was clear: to reduce the complexity of ritual vessels, to introduce more everyday life elements and to restrict the elites through the imposition of strict sumptuary rules. What remains puzzling is why this reform is not mentioned in any written accounts of the history of the Western Zhou, except for some inscriptions mentioning the court's ban on alcohol consumption. One explanation is that it may have been secondary to a much more comprehensive reorganization of elite society, so that it penetrated so deeply into society that even historians with sharp eyes failed to notice it.

3-SECOND SURVEY

Through a series of reforms in bronze production that played a central role in the state, the late Western Zhou court managed to re-establish ritual and social order.

3-MINUTE EXCAVATION

The prominent Chinese bronze specialist, Jessica Rawson, was the first scholar to spot these changes and 'study them as indicators of a major historical phenomenon'. Focusing on the amazing discovery of the famous Zhuangbai No.1 bronze hoard, in which bronzes with distinctive period styles were preserved, she and other scholars were able to reconstruct a complete chronology of these bronzes, with the help of inscriptions, and pin down when these dramatic changes occurred.

RELATED HISTORIES

See also
ZHOUYUAN
page 42

PIECE-MOULD CASTING
page 56

RITUAL VESSELS & THEIR
DISTRIBUTION
page 602

THE SHAN FAMILY
page 62

3-SECOND BIOGRAPHY
JESSICA RAWSON
1943–
Prominent art historian, curator and academic administrator, specializing in Chinese art and archaeology.

30-SECOND TEXT
Yijie Zhuang

Intricately decorated wine vessels were replaced by artefacts based on simple food containers.

SCIENCE & SOCIETY

Bian-stone therapy the treatment of especially neck and back pain by the application of sharpened or heated stones to the affected areas. This is one of the oldest medical therapies in human history, and involves scraping and sometimes piercing the skin, a precursor to acupuncture. It is based on the idea that there is a flow of energy through the body via channels called meridians, and that this flow can become blocked or unbalanced, leading to pain and illness.

commodity coinage a system of currency that uses objects that are perceived to have value in themselves, as opposed to representative currency which stands as a token for something else. Historically, commodity money has included such items as salt, peppercorns, gold, tobacco, cowrie shells, stones and beads.

concubine a woman who has a long-term sexual relationship with a man without being married to him. In Bronze Age China concubines were usually inferior in status to wives, but their children could become heirs, and a chief function of concubinage was to increase the probability that a man would produce a male heir.

conjunction in astronomy, the apparent close approach of two celestial bodies as viewed from the earth. Such conjunctions could be interpreted in the ancient world as having significance for human affairs on earth, and their recording in documents offers a means of dating particular events.

firing method of strengthening, hardening and fixing the shape of a ceramic object by the application of high temperatures.

horn cupping the application of hollow cups to the skin as a form of medical therapy. The first cups were made of horn, although cups could also be made of bamboo or ceramics. The cup was heated to warm the air inside it and then placed on the skin. As the air cooled after it was placed on the body, the change in air pressure inside the cup would draw the skin and the subcutaneous muscle beneath it upwards.

kaolin a soft, earthy, usually white clay mineral, the main component in the manufacture of porcelain. It takes its name from a village called Kao-Ling near the city of Jingdezhen in Jiangxi province, which has been a centre of porcelain manufacture for over 2,000 years.

proto-porcelain an early form of fired and glazed ceramic ware, but without the translucency of true porcelain. Proto-porcelain has been found dating from the Shang dynasty, around 1600 BCE.

silk textile created from the fibrous cocoons of the mulberry silkworm, *Bombyx mori*. Silk fabrics were developed in China perhaps as early as 5000 BCE, and it became one of the most important trade goods in the ancient world. Silk was a luxury fabric that was originally reserved for the Chinese elites.

FOOD

the 30-second history

Five grains – foxtail millet,

common millet, rice, wheat and soya bean – were the staple food of the people living in Bronze Age China. Foxtail millet and common millet were dominant in the north, while rice played a central role in the diet of people in the south. Cooking in the Bronze Age mainly involved the boiling and steaming of grains, though evidence of noodles and cakes has also been found in the marginal areas. While different types of livestock and poultry were raised, pork, along with beef, mutton and chicken, were the main sources of meat in this period. Roasting, boiling and steaming were employed in cooking meat. The Bronze Age Chinese also consumed various vegetables, such as garlic, chives and celery. Wild resources acquired through hunting, gathering and fishing offered a supplementary source of nutrition. The emergence of various types of food triggered the development of specialized cooking, serving and drinking vessels, both ceramic and bronze. Additionally, chopsticks, spoons, knives and forks also appeared as essential utensils in this period. Icehouses identified at several palace sites might have been used to preserve food for the elites; the common people, however, would store their food in cellars or big jars.

3-SECOND SURVEY
Agriculture and animal raising supplied food for people in the Bronze Age, and the prototype of Chinese cuisine had already emerged.

3-MINUTE EXCAVATION
Ancient foodstuffs are occasionally preserved in some specific context, thus expanding our knowledge of the Bronze Age diet. In a Warring States tomb in Shaanxi province, the remains of soup were found in a bronze tripod, and a bone in it was identified to be from a dog. Another interesting discovery came from the Subeixi cemetery in Xinjiang, where noodles and cakes were discovered and the analysis revealed that they were made of common millet.

RELATED HISTORIES
See also
ALCOHOL
page 78

30-SECOND TEXT
Siran Liu

The ancient Chinese diet was based on the cultivation of grains, though they also raised animals for meat.

ALCOHOL

the 30-second history

The Bronze Age witnessed the

development of alcohol-making in China. Alcohol in this period can be divided into two main categories, *li* and *jiu*. *Li* was brewed using sprouted grain, while *jiu* used distiller's yeast. The two types of alcohol were consumed at different occasions and events. *Li* was mainly used in sacrificial practices as an offering to the gods and ancestors, while *jiu* was for daily drinking. The most significant evidence for the highly developed alcohol-making system in this period is the complex assemblages of bronze wine containers and drinking vessels. In Shang elite tombs, the most important burial goods were sets of these wine vessels, such as *zun*, *jue* and *gu*, which outnumbered even the food containers. The main ingredient for alcohol was grain, specifically rice, and the highly developed drinking culture of this period probably indicates a large agricultural surplus (although it might also be the case that production was monopolized by the minority elites). Excessive drinking could be blamed for the collapse of the early kingdoms. The last kings of the Xia and Shang dynasties were both accused of constructing massive wine pools, large enough to sail boats on. The early kings of the Zhou dynasty restricted the consumption of alcohol, though it was still widely used in ritual ceremonies and feasts.

3-SECOND SURVEY
Alcohol-making was highly developed in the Bronze Age of China and played a significant role in both ritual practice and the daily life of ancient people.

3-MINUTE EXCAVATION
In an early Western Zhou cemetery excavated in 2013 at the site of Shigushan in Shaanxi province, a bronze *you* vessel still containing alcohol was found in an elite tomb. This is currently the earliest material evidence of alcohol in China. Many other bronze wine vessels, such as *zun*, *hu*, *zhi* and *jin* were found in the same tomb and might have been used as a set with the *you* for wine drinking.

RELATED HISTORIES
See also
RITUAL VESSELS &
THEIR DISTRIBUTION
page 60

30-SECOND TEXT
Siran Liu

Alcohol was of central importance to ritual, as evidenced by the variety of drinking vessels found in elite tombs.

POTTERY PRODUCTION

the 30-second history

Although ceramics were no longer the major focus of craft production in the Bronze Age, pottery manufacture did not cease. The production of ceramics and bronzes were closely tied together, and continuous innovations were beneficial to both industries. With their mastery of high-temperature firing, the Late Neolithic people in China had realized that some minerals could be turned into a fluid glaze to coat the surface of ceramics. This glazing technology was more widely used in the Bronze Age to produce so-called proto-porcelain to satisfy the elites' new obsession with objects with lustrous surfaces. The Bronze Age people in south and southeast China were excellent makers of this proto-porcelain. With their great technological achievements in bronze casting, the Shang were capable of transforming ordinary clay into stunning pieces. They found out that a certain type of kaolin is perfect for producing white ceramics on which beautiful decorations could be displayed. In Lady Fu Hao's tomb, a huge number of white ceramics were placed, along with numerous bronze items and stone and jade objects. These ceramics and some of the stone artefacts mimicked the forms of the bronzes. For the Bronze Age elites, the forms and shapes of different kinds of objects could be freely and fluidly transformed from one to another.

3-SECOND SURVEY
Closely related to bronze casting, pottery production continued to flourish during the Bronze Age.

3-MINUTE EXCAVATION
A breakthrough in research on proto-porcelain came about with the discovery of the Yue state elite tombs in Hongshan, Jiangsu province. Each tomb contains hundreds, if not thousands of objects, the majority of which are proto-porcelain in the same shapes as bronze ritual vessels and musical instruments. Some of the earliest glass was also discovered. With its shining surfaces and beautiful decoration, this glazed proto-porcelain represents the highest level of ceramic production of this period.

RELATED HISTORIES
See also
ERLITOU
page 32

YINXU
page 34

PIECE-MOULD CASTING
page 56

3-SECOND BIOGRAPHY
FU HAO
died c. 1200 BCE
Posthumous title of Mu Xin, the consort of King Wu Ding, famous for being a female military general. Her tomb was excavated in 1976, generating the largest number of burial objects of any Bronze Age elite tomb.

30-SECOND TEXT
Yijie Zhuang

Ancient Chinese ceramics ranged from simple domestic vessels to lustrous glazed proto-porcelain.

TEXTILES
& CLOTHING

the 30-second history

Because of their organic nature, ancient textiles rarely survive. Most of the examples we have come from sealed tomb contexts and from textile impressions identified from corrosion imprints on bronze objects in tombs. The most significant aspect of the Chinese textile industry was the invention of silk, the use of which reached its artistic zenith in the Eastern Zhou period (771–221 BCE). Tomb 1 of the Chu state at Mashan (4th century BCE) in Hubei province yielded the best-known archaeological finds of silk textiles. The deceased was fully dressed before being wrapped in 13 layers of beautifully decorated garments and coverlets. Their sheer textures and brilliant colours provide material evidence about the development of Chinese textile manufacture – silk-weaving structures and pattern techniques, birds and dragons as major decorative motifs, and embroidered ornamentation. The most common articles of clothing were robes of different lengths. Disparity in clothing materials was a mark of social status, as silk was exclusive to the elites, in contrast to the hemp clothing worn by others. During the Zhou dynasty, systems of colour and design on outfits were gradually developed to distinguish different social classes, and this was adopted by later dynasties.

3-SECOND SURVEY
The complicated procedures, vast resources and immense labour and time required to produce textiles, especially silk, made them a fundamental element of a privileged lifestyle in ancient China.

3-MINUTE EXCAVATION
The unique Chu tomb structures contributed significantly to the miraculous preservation of silk textiles. In a typical Chu burial, wooden coffins were covered by layers of charcoal and thick white clay, and buried deep underground. These painstaking efforts to insulate the tomb guaranteed a stable temperature and humidity in the chambers, and effectively sealed the tomb from penetration by oxygen and bacteria, thus aiding the preservation of organic materials.

RELATED HISTORIES
See also
DECORATION & SOCIAL MEANINGS
page 68

30-SECOND TEXT
Qin Cao

The ancient Chinese were skilled in the production of textiles, most especially silk, and their designs developed into a sophisticated indicator of social hierarchies.

One of the earliest recorded Chinese physicians, according to legend Bian Que was a gifted diagnostician and his skills ranged from acupuncture to surgery.

BIAN QUE

Bian Que was the medical officer of the legendary Emperor Huang, though his dates are a matter of dispute. The first doctor mentioned in historical texts, he was adept at surgery, gynaecology and paediatrics, but particularly at pulse taking and acupuncture. Bian Que emphasized the importance of communication with and observation of patients, as these were an efficient means of accurate diagnosis in an age without scientific equipment. It was said that he could judge the condition of a patient from his very first glance. He once paid a visit to Qi Huan Gong (Duke Huan of Qi state, died 643 BCE) and told him that he was slightly ill and should be treated quickly. Qi Huan Gong did not listen. Bian Que visited him every couple of days subsequently and warned him that his disease had gradually progressed from skin, to blood, to gastrointestinal tract. On his last visit, Bian Que said it was too late for Qi Huan Gong to be cured. Sure enough, Qi Huan Gong died shortly afterwards.

Another time Bian Que was on his way to the capital of Guo state when he heard that the prince of Guo had died suddenly. He asked about the prince's symptoms and suggested that it was just shock rather than death. The prince's attendants checked his body according to Bian Que's advice and found that the prince was still breathing and his body warm. Afterwards, they invited Bian Que to the palace to save the prince's life.

However, according to historical records, Guo state was defunct hundreds of years before the reign of Qi Huan Gong, so Bian Que could not have attended both the prince of Guo and Duke Huan. A solution to this puzzle was suggested in 2013, when a batch of bamboo slips were discovered in a Han dynasty tomb in Sichuan province. Most of the slips were medical books, including one entitled *Medical Theory of Bi Xi*. Experts think that 'Bi Xi' was the ancient pronunciation of 'Bian Que'. Thus, these books might be the classics written by the 'Bian Que School' of the Eastern Zhou period. They had been using the title 'Bian Que' for several hundred years, and so the Bian Que who saved the life of the Guo prince might be a different person from the one who saw Qi Huan Gong in 643 BCE.

Chao Tang & Yijie Zhuang

COINAGE

the 30-second history

Most transactions in the Early Bronze Age of China were performed using commodities as currency. The emergence of a true monetary system had to wait until the Eastern Zhou period. By then, the states of central-north China employed three main types of bronze coinage, which still bore the shape of primitive commodity currencies. They were the spade-shaped *Bu* coin, the knife-shaped *Dao* coin and rounded coins with a round or square hole in the middle. In south China, the coinage system was quite different, possibly indicating a different trajectory of cultural development. The area of ancient Chu, while also using *Bu* coins, operated largely with *Yi Bi* coins, which were usually perforated, shell-shaped and had pronounced inscriptions on the front surface. The shape might have been derived from the ancient tradition of using shells and shell-shaped bronze as currency. Precious metal coinage, such as the gold stamped plaque, also appeared during this period, though it played a relatively minor role compared to the bronze coinages. When the first emperor, Qin Shinghuandi, finally united the country in 221 BCE, he adopted the round coin called *Ban Liang* as the currency of his empire. This became the prototype for almost all Chinese bronze coins in later periods.

3-SECOND SURVEY
The early metallic coinages of ancient China appeared first in the Eastern Zhou period, imitating the forms of common daily artefacts and commodities.

3-MINUTE EXCAVATION
Despite the large quantities of Eastern Zhou coins that have been excavated, the widespread exchange of these coins between different areas makes it difficult to determine in which state they were produced. Hence the identification of coin-casting foundries becomes very significant. The casting foundries in Luoyang, the Eastern Zhou capital city, for instance, revealed a special type of mould for casting socketed spade-shaped Bu coins, suggesting that this coinage might have been issued by the Eastern Zhou kings.

3-SECOND BIOGRAPHIES
EMPEROR QINSHIHUANG
260–210 BCE
The first emperor of China.

30-SECOND TEXT
Siran Liu

The earliest Chinese coins retained the shapes of recognizable objects such as knives and rings.

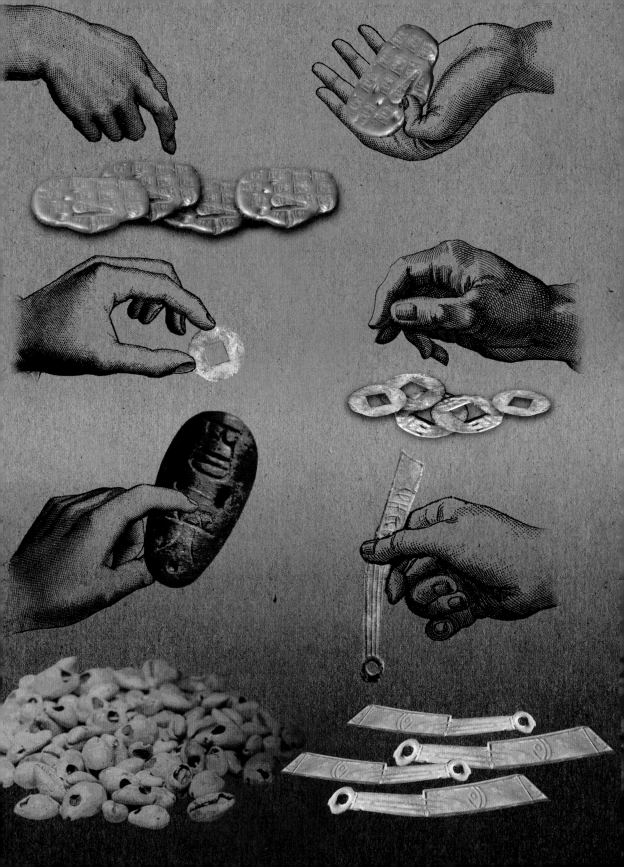

ASTRONOMY & THE CALENDAR

the 30-second history

The Shang calendar was derived from observations of the movements of the sun and moon, which were noted and charted. Solar and lunar eclipses were also observed, and oracle bone divination records include predictions of such events, which were believed to signify good or bad fortune. The most famous example of this was related to the Zhou's conquest of the Shang in the 11th century BCE. The observation of the conjunction of the first visible planets was taken as a propitious sign for the Zhou's forthcoming military campaign. The recording of this astronomical phenomenon gave important evidence for the modern reconstruction of the chronology of the Bronze Age. The Shang calendar was made up of 60-day cycles. Each day had a name that combined two different number sequences, called the 10 heavenly stems and the 12 earthly branches. A month followed the movement of the moon, which is either 29 or 30 days, and a year consisted of 12 lunar months, with an extra month added every three years to bring the calendar back into step with the solar year. The calendar was closely associated with the reigning power. On an oracle bone inscription, a year was commonly recorded as, for example, 'the king's fifth year'. This tradition was followed by chroniclers throughout the royal dynasties. The lunar calendar is still used in China for agricultural work and traditional festivals.

3-SECOND SURVEY
Astronomy and the calendar were closely linked to significant aspects of Bronze Age societies, in particular warfare, ritual offerings and sacrifices, and agriculture.

3-MINUTE EXCAVATION
The popularity and prominence of astronomy in the Bronze Age has been attested by archaeological discoveries in the 20th century. One example is the decoration on a lacquer box lid from an elite tomb, that of Marquis Yi of Zeng in Suixian, Hubei province. A depiction of the Northern Dipper is surrounded by the inscribed names of the complete sequence of the 28 stellar lodges.

RELATED HISTORIES
See also
SUIZHOU ZENG MARQUIS CEMETERY
page 44

DIVINATION & SHAMANISM
page 104

HUMAN & ANIMAL SACRIFICES
page 108

ORACLE BONE INSCRIPTIONS
page 116

3-SECOND BIOGRAPHY
MARQUIS YI OF ZENG
died c. 433 BCE
Ruler of the Zeng state, Warring States period.

30-SECOND TEXT
Qin Cao

The ancient Chinese related astronomical observations to earthly events such as harvests and battles.

MARRIAGE, GENDER & CHILDREN

the 30-second history

Our earliest information about marriage in ancient China comes from inscriptions on oracle bones, although the documentation is limited to social elites. From the way that women are named in these inscriptions, it has been deduced that monogamy was the custom during the early Shang period, while polygamy became the dominant practice during the later Shang. During the middle Western Zhou period monogamy again became the norm, though it was customary for a husband to have several concubines. Marriage between couples with the same family name was forbidden from this period. Marriages began to be recorded through inscriptions on bronze vessels, which show that feudal princes used marriage to cement alliances. However, the core function of marriage in the Bronze Age was to continue the family line via sons, and the increased number of consorts after the early Shang period was probably to ensure the birth of male offspring. Women appear in documents with their surnames only after marriage, and before marriage they are rarely recorded and never named, implying that their roles in society were largely bound up with their husbands. The consorts of the Shang kings frequently participated in ritual ceremonies and warfare, but in the Zhou period women withdrew from any kind of social activity and were largely constrained by ethical codes.

30-SECOND TEXT
Siran Liu

3-SECOND SURVEY
Marriage, gender and children were closely associated in the Chinese Bronze Age. A woman gained her social role via marriage while the core function of marriage was to produce male offspring to continue the family line.

3-MINUTE EXCAVATION
Although most women had quite restricted roles in Zhou society, exceptions did exist. When a high-born woman married a powerful lord, she could be influential. For instance, the sister of King Xiang of Zhou married Duke Xiang of Song state, and became the stepmother and stepgrandmother of two later dukes. She seized power in the Song court for long periods, and even plotted the murder of her stepgrandson, Duke Zhao, to allow another stepgrandson and her secret lover, *Bao*, to become Duke Wen.

The inscription on this bronze vessel from the Western Zhou period records the alliance made between the states of Deng and Ying, which was solemnized by the marriage for which the vessel formed part of the dowry.

MEDICINE

the 30-second history

The ancient medicine of China, which stemmed from prehistoric witchcraft, developed significantly during the Bronze Age. By the Shang period, more than 30 diseases relating to different parts of the body had been recorded in the oracle bone inscriptions. Healers could not only diagnose various illnesses based on different symptoms, they could also predict the trends of illnesses by monitoring the disease's progress and employ corresponding therapeutic methods. Besides herbal medicines, Bian-stone therapy (the precursor of acupuncture) and simple surgery had also been developed. Nonetheless, most healing activities in Shang society still had a quasi-magical nature, and the first medical professionals did not emerge until the late Western Zhou period. The Eastern Zhou period witnessed a major development in diagnostic techniques and methods of treatment. Various herbs began to be used in compounds to enhance their healing effects. Other methods such as massage, baths, acupuncture and horn cupping were also employed in medical treatment. More fundamentally, a theoretical system interweaving practical medical knowledge and traditional philosophies was established, which laid the foundation for traditional Chinese medicine as we know it today. Famous doctors of the period, such as Bian Que, were recorded in historical documents along with classical prescriptions.

3-SECOND SURVEY
Traditional Chinese medicine was initiated in the Shang and Western Zhou periods, and was fully developed in the Eastern Zhou period.

3-MINUTE EXCAVATION
The earliest confirmed evidence of medical instruments and herbal medicine was found at the site of Taixi in Gaocheng, Hebei province. Among the burial goods of a tomb dated to the Shang period, a Bian-stone was found in a lacquered box. In the remains of a house on the same site, various seeds were found in different ceramic jars, some of which might have been used to treat diarrhoea.

RELATED HISTORIES
See also
BIAN QUE
page 84

30-SECOND TEXT
Siran Liu

Traditional Chinese herbal medicine as we know it has its roots in the Bronze Age's philosophical systems.

AFTERLIFE & BELIEFS

chamber in a Chinese Bronze Age tomb, an outer coffin of timber or sometimes brick, within which might be an inner coffin of timber.

demographics the quantifiable statistics of a given population, such as age range, gender balance, ethnicity, social status, etc.

Neolithic the Neolithic period in China dates from c. 8500–3000 BCE, though these dates remain a matter of debate. The earliest Neolithic culture so far discovered in China is the Nanzhuangtou in present-day Hebei province. The Neolithic period saw the beginnings of crop cultivation and animal domestication and the use of polished stone tools.

jade this is the name for two types of metamorphic rock, nephrite and jadeite; nephrite was the stone used for various decorative purposes in Bronze Age China. Nephrite can be a creamy-white or various shades of green, and nephrite deposits in China were mined as early as 6000 BCE.

pyromancy the art of divination using fire.

ritual a sequence of activities usually carried out in a religious context, which may involve specific words or actions, and is usually characterized by invariance, fixed forms and deference to tradition. In the Chinese Bronze Age central control of ritual was a means of maintaining the power and status of elites. The use of bronze vessels of different types characterized ritual in Bronze Age China. The evolution of such ritual vessels over time offers one method of interpreting and periodizing social and cultural changes.

shaft-pit tomb type of tomb consisting of an underground pit dug into the earth, with a lining of timber or sometimes brick forming a burial chamber. Access would be via steps or a ramp, and a mound would be raised above the chamber.

shaman person believed to be able to access and influence the spirit world, often by means of rituals or the attainment of trancelike states. Shamans are often credited with powers of healing or divination.

sumptuary laws set of regulations that control the consumption of especially luxury goods, usually by stipulating that particular foods, or clothes or materials could only be used by higher social classes. Sumptuary laws were instituted as a means of establishing and maintaining social hierarchies.

vassal state a state that is subordinate to another. During the Zhou dynasty there were a number of states that recognized the authority of the Zhou court and supplied military assistance when requested. Some were little more than fortified towns, but others controlled significant amounts of territory and enjoyed a degree of autonomy.

waist-pit a sacrificial pit beneath a coffin in which sacrificial animals were usually found.

TOMBS OF THE SHANG ELITES

the 30-second history

The tombs of late Shang elites discovered at Yinxu (Anyang) can be classified into three categories: Shang royal burials, high-status tombs and medium or low-rank elite tombs in cemeteries distributed throughout the capital. During the 1930s, the excavations at the Xibeigang cemetery uncovered a total of 14 tombs with ramps, alongside over 800 sacrificial pits. As the number of ramps associated with a tomb is viewed as an indicator of status, the eight 4-ramp burials in the cemetery – which are unparalleled in terms of their size, the number of human or animal sacrifices interred inside the chambers and the number of sacrificial pits associated with them – are usually attributed to the Shang kings. Unfortunately, most of these royal tombs have been extensively looted over the years. The tomb of Fu Hao, a consort of King Wu Ding, was the first undisturbed high-rank burial to be discovered at Anyang. Her tomb included more than 1,600 kg (1.75 tons) of bronzes, over 700 pieces of jade and other prestige goods made of exotic materials, such as ivory cups and marble and turquoise objects. Lower-rank elite tombs were also found in various parts of Yinxu. Spatially, the cemeteries are often subdivided into different clusters that show consistency in terms of burial goods and emblems on bronzes, and these were possibly occupied by different lineages.

RELATED HISTORIES
See also
HUMAN & ANIMAL SACRIFICES
page 108

THE USE OF JADE
page 110

3-SECOND SURVEY
Elite tombs of the late Shang offer valuable evidence regarding mortuary systems, elite craft industries and, in particular, social organization.

3-MINUTE EXCAVATION
Late Shang elite tombs have also been widely found outside of Anyang. These tombs usually exhibit certain indigenous funeral practices, while including Yinxu-style mortuary goods. The occupants of these tombs might have been regional allies or agents of the Shang state taking charge of resources or tribute transportation. In other words, the late Shang appeared to rely on religion or ideology to maintain their large political and trade network.

3-SECOND BIOGRAPHIES
FU HAO
died c. 1200 BCE
The consort of King Wu Ding, famous for being a military general. Her tomb was excavated in 1976, generating the largest number of burial objects of any Bronze Age elite tomb.

WU DING
reigned c. 1250–1192 BCE
A king of the Shang dynasty

30-SECOND TEXT
Wengcheong Lam

The tomb of Lady Fu Hao yielded a magnificent array of prestige objects from the Bronze Age. The image at right shows a reconstruction of the tomb.

STATE CEMETERIES OF THE ZHOU

the 30-second history

To control its vast territory, the Western Zhou established significant numbers of vassal states in the Central Plains and parts of the Yangtze valley. The majority of these states were ruled by Zhou kin branches. Since the 1980s, archaeological work has identified at least ten Zhou vassal states (e.g. Jin and Yan) and about a dozen non-Zhou vassal states through the excavation of their cemeteries. The discoveries are significant for an understanding of two aspects of Western Zhou politics. First, they help clarify how social rank was structured. In each cemetery, lords and their lineages were usually buried in a cluster separate from the commoners; the layout of the Jin Marquis cemetery is the best example of this. These elite members were buried with sets of bronze vessels, musical instruments, chariots, jade ornaments, etc., to demonstrate their power over sacrificial ritual and administration. Second, aspects of the materials used illustrate the organization of the political network. For instance, bronzes from the state cemeteries show a high degree of similarity to their counterparts from the capital area, the Wei river valley. However, daily-used ceramics in regional centres are different from the assemblages in the capital area. Thus the sovereignty of the Zhou over their vassal states was achieved primarily through transporting elite culture from the core to the peripheries.

3-SECOND SURVEY
The state cemeteries of the Western Zhou provide tangible evidence of how the dynasty laid the foundations of the early Chinese empire.

3-MINUTE EXCAVATION
Non-Zhou vassal states fall into three categories: the political alliances of the Zhou court in the capital area (evidenced by the Yu state cemetery in Baoji, Shaanxi); descendants of the Shang family (e.g. the Changzikou tomb in Luyi, Henan); and societies living on the periphery of the Western Zhou polity (e.g. the Peng state cemetery in Jiangxiang, Shanxi). The cemeteries of these states usually present distinctive practices such as waist-pits, human or animal sacrifices, and the burial of exotic bronzes, elements that are often absent from cemeteries belonging to Zhou elites.

RELATED HISTORIES
See also
SUIZHOU ZENG MARQUIS CEMETERY
page 44

TOMBS OF THE SHANG ELITES
page 98

COMMONER BURIALS
page 102

30-SECOND TEXT
Wengcheong Lam

Funerary objects help explain how elite culture was transmitted from the dynastic centre to the vassal regions.

COMMONER BURIALS

the 30-second history

During the Shang and Zhou

periods commoners were buried in cemeteries at many locations in the capital area or in urban centres, together with lower-rank elites. These burials are usually shaft-pit tombs and include simple pottery assemblages, but without wooden chambers, jade amulets or bronze objects such as weapons. Commoner cemeteries of the Bronze Age were usually subdivided into several sectors, and in each sector tombs were concentrated and separated from other burial plots. The orientation, body position and type of burial goods in each sector show a relatively high similarity, indicating that the burials belonged to the same lineage or kin-group. It is notable that, throughout the entire Bronze Age, infants were buried separately in residential areas or near houses, and not with adults in the cemeteries. These burials usually do not include any burial goods or even wooden coffins. Furthermore, unlike the high elites, there is no solid evidence that the practice of joint burials of husbands and wives in separate pits was adopted among commoners until the very end of the Bronze Age. This indicates that the layout and arrangement of commoner cemeteries may have focused more on reinforcing the preoccupation with lineage relationships instead of the smaller individual family units.

3-SECOND SURVEY
Although commoner burials do not yield any remarkable burial goods, they can give important clues in understanding the horizontal social structure (i.e., kinship relations) as well as the vertical hierarchy or social ranking.

3-MINUTE EXCAVATION
The best evidence for documenting the demographics of commoner social groups comes from the Shangma cemetery, which includes more than 1,387 tombs and was the first cemetery to be excavated almost completely. According to Lothar von Falkenhausen's work, during the middle Spring- and Autumn period the community had a population of between 380 and 750 people – who may have belonged to the same kin-based lineage including both elites or leaders and common members.

RELATED HISTORIES
See also
SUIZHOU ZENG MARQUIS CEMETERY
page 44

TOMBS OF THE SHANG ELITES
page 98

STATE CEMETERIES OF THE ZHOU
page 100

30-SECOND TEXT
Wengcheong Lam

Commoners were buried with simple objects, but had the same desire to enter the afterlife properly equipped.

DIVINATION & SHAMANISM

the 30-second history

3-SECOND SURVEY

During the Late Shang period, divination became a state-sponsored ritual controlled exclusively by the kings and a small group of diviners who were trained in literacy and the relevant ritual procedures.

3-MINUTE EXCAVATION

The logic behind the divination process in the late Shang period lies in the fact the Shang kings were the only channels of communication with the ancestral spirits. These could intercede with the highest deity, Ti, to provide favourable consequences like a fruitful harvest or assistance in warfare, once they had received the proper number of sacrificial offerings provided by the correct type of rituals on the right day.

Divination was one important means by which the late Shang kings established their rule and authority. The practice of pyromantic divination using scapulars began as early as the Neolithic period in East Asia, but the systematic preparation of bones or turtle shells by trimming, polishing, drilling and chiselling a series of oval and circular holes to obtain a regular shape of cracks was a significant invention of the late Shang, probably associated with King Wu Ding. The elaboration of divination processes may have provided a means of monopolizing and restricting the knowledge of ritual to the Shang kings and a small group of diviners. A heated metal stick was used to burn holes and make cracks on prepared bones, and the king was then responsible for interpreting the meaning of the cracks, which would address a wide range of questions from the result of a military campaign to agricultural harvests. Thereafter the question addressed, the prognostication and in some cases the verification of the result would be carved into the bone or turtle shell. Divination was a defining feature of Shang politics, and the Shang kings are often referred to as 'shamans' in scholarly work, because they were able to communicate with the ancestral dead with the help of animals and a series of religious ceremonies.

RELATED HISTORIES

See also
ORACLE BONE INSCRIPTIONS
page 116

3-SECOND BIOGRAPHY

WU DING
reigned c. 1250–1192 BCE
A king of the Shang dynasty

30-SECOND TEXT

Wengcheong Lam

Patterned ox bones and turtle shells were the most commonly used objects for pyromantic divination.

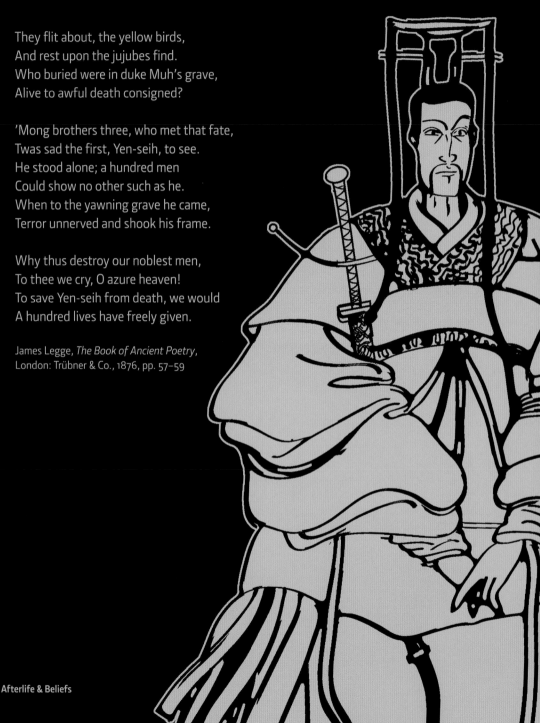

They flit about, the yellow birds,
And rest upon the jujubes find.
Who buried were in duke Muh's grave,
Alive to awful death consigned?

'Mong brothers three, who met that fate,
Twas sad the first, Yen-seih, to see.
He stood alone; a hundred men
Could show no other such as he.
When to the yawning grave he came,
Terror unnerved and shook his frame.

Why thus destroy our noblest men,
To thee we cry, O azure heaven!
To save Yen-seih from death, we would
A hundred lives have freely given.

James Legge, *The Book of Ancient Poetry*,
London: Trübner & Co., 1876, pp. 57–59

QIN MU GONG

Composed nearly 2,500 years ago, the poem opposite describes the tragic deaths of three noble brothers of Qin state, who were human sacrifices of their monarch, Qin Mu Gong (Duke Mu of Qin state, r. 659–621 BCE). The territory of Qin had been very close to the Western Zhou capital, but this territory was no longer prosperous after the chaotic decline of the Western Zhou dynasty. Qin and its people, surrounded by the Xirong and other ethnic minorities, were considered barbarians by the states to the east of the Yellow river after the eastern migration of the Zhou royal court.

However, Qin Mu Gong conquered several minority tribes during his reign and expanded his western territory, which made Qin state the overlord of the west land. As a man with charisma, Qin Mu Gong treasured talented people. He brought back Bailixi, a slave of Chu, at a cost of five pieces of sheepskin, and made him prime minister. Despite opposition from his ministers, he trusted General Meng Ming Shi, who had twice been defeated by the Jin. With his support, Meng eventually defeated the powerful Jin army.

Another dramatic story showed his character: a thoroughbred horse escaped from his paddock and was killed and eaten by some peasants. The protector of the horses arrested 300 peasants and sentenced them to death. Hearing of this event, Qin Mu Gong said: 'Men of high character should cherish lives more than property. I have heard that eating good horsemeat without drinking is harmful to the health, so reward the peasants with good wine and free them.' Later, when fighting against the Jin, Qin Mu Gong was injured and trapped in an impasse. The 300 peasants he had spared risked their lives to rescue him.

After Qin Mu Gong's death, over 170 people were buried alive with him. Many of them were noble ministers. This event destroyed the elite of Qin state, and led to continuous instability throughout the Spring-and-Autumn period.

Chao Tang & Yijie Zhuang

Duke Mu of Qin (Qin Mu Gong) was a charismatic leader who succeeded in expanding the territory of the Qin state. This depiction shows him wearing a later style of dress.

HUMAN & ANIMAL SACRIFICES

the 30-second history

Human and animal sacrifices

were a significant component of various rituals throughout the Chinese Bronze Age. Sacrificial pits containing human and animal remains were already widespread during the Longshan period, known as the transitional period before the Bronze Age. The practice of sacrificing humans and animals as offerings in a wide range of contexts – including burials, storage pits and palace foundations – witnessed a dramatic increase during the Erlitou and early Shang periods, and reached its peak in the late Shang period. The most illustrative example is the Xibeigang royal cemetery, where at least 30,000 human victims were sacrificed in rituals. After the founding of the Western Zhou dynasty, the practice of human sacrificial offerings was gradually abandoned, but the role of animal sacrifices in rituals remained important. For instance, animal sacrifices served as a critical element of funeral rituals performed at the cemeteries of the Jin marquises at Tianma-Qucun and Yangshe, Shaanxi, both during and after the time of burial. In addition, rows of sacrificial pits containing the remains of sheep/goats, cattle and humans have been found in the central courtyard of the Majiazhuang palace in Fengxiang, Shaanxi, which is considered to be an ancestral temple of the rulers of the Qin state during the Eastern Zhou.

3-SECOND SURVEY
Sacrificial ritual served as the foundation for elite authority and played a crucial role in the construction of political leadership.

3-MINUTE EXCAVATION
As sacrificial rituals were performed on a grand scale, the late Shang diviners developed a wide vocabulary for the ways of killing sacrifices, like beheading, splitting into halves, chopping, burning and burying, as demonstrated by this inscription: 'Making-cracks on *jimao day*, Que divined: "In performing the exorcism for Lady Hao to Father Yi, [we] cleave a sheep and a pig and pledge ten penned sheep."' (*Heji* 271f)

RELATED HISTORIES
See also
TOMBS OF THE SHANG ELITES
page 98

STATE CEMETERIES
OF THE ZHOU
page 100

ORACLE BONE INSCRIPTIONS
page 116

30-SECOND TEXT
Wengcheong Lam

These skeletal remains from an early Shang period sacrificial pit at Zhengzhou indicate the scale of the practice of human and animal sacrifices.

THE USE OF JADE

the 30-second history

The tradition of using jade (nephrite) for ornaments and its associated craft technology has deep historical roots that can be traced back to the late Neolithic cultures. Starting from the Early Bronze Age, this practice became more ritualized and integrated into the state-controlled ceremonies. At the Erlitou site, for instance, jade knives, axes, *ge* halberds, *gui* ceremonial blades and turquoise inlaid objects were buried in richly equipped tombs with bronze ritual vessels and ornaments. This indicates that jade objects were highly valued in mortuary ceremonies and represented the concept that, in the afterlife, the dead would require everything they had used when alive. The large amount of jade found in the tomb of Lady Fu Hao offers an important profile of the use of this material in the Shang period: not only has the craftsmanship achieved a high level, but the repertoire has also expanded to include objects like bi discs, rings, bracelets and animal figurines that had not been found in previous elite tombs. Jade was no less significant in the Western Zhou period. The Zhou elites also developed new tastes, preferring geometric and interweaving patterns of motifs; using jade for face-covers to protect the spirits of their ancestors; and combining beads, tubes and plaques to make complex pendant ornaments as a token of grave occupants' high status.

3-SECOND SURVEY
Jade was not only an exotic commodity related to long-distance trade but also an indispensable part of the regalia in various rituals and ceremonies during the Bronze Age.

3-MINUTE EXCAVATION
Antique-style jade objects were frequently found in elite tombs. For instance, the jade collection in the Fu Hao tomb includes items from Neolithic cultures such as the Shijiahe, Liangzhu and Hongshan. Similarly, jade objects dating back to the late Shang or even the Neolithic were found in the marquis tombs of the Jin, Guo and Rui states, indicating that jade objects would have been passed down as heirlooms in elite families.

RELATED HISTORIES
See also
TOMBS OF THE SHANG ELITES
page 98

STATE CEMETERIES
OF THE ZHOU
page 100

LONG-DISTANCE TRADE
page 146

3-SECOND BIOGRAPHY
FU HAO
died c. 1200 BCE
The consort of King Wu Ding, famous for being a military general. Her tomb was excavated in 1976, generating the largest number of burial objects of any Bronze Age elite tomb.

30-SECOND TEXT
Wengcheong Lam

Jade was used to create complex decorative objects, some of which were kept by families for many generations.

WRITING & PHILOSOPHY

WRITING & PHILOSOPHY
GLOSSARY

Agriculturalism an agrarian social and political philosophy based on a form of utopian communalism. The Agriculturalists believed that human beings were in essence farmers, that the ideal ruler worked in the fields alongside his subjects and that society should be based on an egalitarian self-sufficiency. Agriculturalism was suppressed by the Qin dynasty and few of its texts are extant.

epistemology the branch of philosophy concerned with knowledge – what knowledge is, how it can be acquired and what its relation is to concepts such as truth and belief.

ethics the branch of philosophy concerned with identifying, justifying and systematizing codes of right and wrong behaviour.

glyphs in writing, a mark (for example a letter or a symbol) that has meaning in some system of language, such that in association with other glyphs it can express ideas or concepts.

Mohism school of philosophy that developed around the time of Confucianism, which was characterized by a rather austere and utilitarian view of human life, with an emphasis on order and parsimony and a rejection of music and art. Mohists were scientifically minded and technologically skilled, which allowed them to hold significant social and political power, but their ethical positions were largely absorbed by Confucianism, and their political influence waned after China was unified.

Naturalism school of philosophy that explained the universe in terms of the complementary concepts of yin (dark, cold, female, negative) and yang (light, warm, male, positive) and the Five Elements (earth, fire, water, wood, metal). Zou Yan (305–240 BCE) is considered to have been the founder of this school, whose teachings were absorbed by Taoism.

paleography the study of ancient and historical writing in terms of its development, the processes used to create it and its deciphering and dating.

proto-porcelain an early form of fired and glazed ceramic ware, but without the translucency of true porcelain. Proto-porcelain has been found dating from the Shang dynasty, around 1600 BCE.

Warring States period period following on from the Spring-and-Autumn period, 475 BCE to 221 BCE, roughly corresponding to the second part of the Eastern Zhou dynasty. As the Zhou weakened, various smaller states struggled for supremacy, and various alliances and wars took place, culminating in the victory of Qin state and the unification of China under Emperor Qinshihuang in 221 BCE.

ORACLE BONE INSCRIPTIONS

the 30-second history

The significance of inscribed oracle bones was first established in 1899 by Wang Yirong, who recognized that the marks on the bones resembled Chinese characters. The oracle bones examined by Wang were connected with the Yinxu site of the late Shang dynasty. Although these form the bulk of the earliest preserved Chinese written corpus, the script cannot be the actual first writing, since the maturity of the script and its capacity to record complex ideas indicates that the writing system itself is much older. Oracle bones were mainly used for royal divinations. Hollows carved into one side of the bone or shell were scorched by the diviner to cause a pattern of cracks on the other side, from which the oracle would be read in response to the king's question. The inscription, mainly for royal display, was carved after the ritual was complete. Although covering a wide range of social, political, military and economic topics, the inscriptions cannot be relied upon as historically accurate since they were primarily used for ritual purposes. Oracle bones were not exclusive to the Shang kings, since inscribed divination bones have also been associated with Shang non-royals, contemporary neighbours from Zhengzhou in the south and Daxinzhuang in the east, as well as with Zhou people in the Wei river valley both before and after their conquest of the Shang.

RELATED HISTORIES
See also
YINXU
page 34

BRONZE INSCRIPTIONS
page 118

3-SECOND SURVEY
Although the use of bone divination may date back to the Neolithic period (c. 6500–5500 BCE), the practice of carving inscriptions on bones or shells seems to have begun in the reign of Wu Ding, c. 1200 BCE.

3-MINUTE EXCAVATION
Most of the bone and shell inscriptions known to us bear only a few characters. A lengthier text concerns the pregnancy of Lady Fu Hao, the wife of Wu Ding. It reads: 'Crack- making on the day *jiashen*, Que divines: "Will Lady Hao's childbearing be lucky?" The king predicts: "If the child is born on a *ding* day, it will be lucky; if on a *geng* day, greatly favourable." Three weeks and one day later, on the day *jiayin*, the child was born. Not lucky. It was a girl.' *Jiayin* was neither a *ding* nor a *geng* day, so the king was right.

3-SECOND BIOGRAPHY
WANG YIRONG
1845–1900
President of the Imperial University, was an expert on traditional studies of metal and stone inscriptions, and the first to collect oracle bones.

30-SECOND TEXT
Peng Peng

Wang Yirong recognized that the marks on bone fragments resembled inscriptions found on stone and metal.

BRONZE INSCRIPTIONS

the 30-second history

The earliest bronze inscriptions are preserved on Shang vessels dating to the reign of Wu Ding around 1200 BCE. Most of these consist of an emblem or an ancestor dedication, and have fluent curving strokes consistent with contemporary brush writing. During the last two Shang reigns (c. 11th century BCE), a few examples begin to include narrative texts in which the vessel-maker informs his deceased ancestor of a reward he has received. These could be viewed as prototypes of similar Western Zhou bronze texts. Compared with the late Shang examples, Western Zhou inscriptions are remarkably lengthy and varied in content, covering a vast range of topics such as official appointments, military merits, marriages and economic activities. However, because of the religious context of ancestor worship, bronze texts have to be used cautiously as historical evidence. In the Eastern Zhou period, following the decline of the Zhou royal house and great social transformations, certain terms (e.g., *tianzi*, 'Son of Heaven', a reference to the Zhou king) and formulaic expressions (e.g., the dedicatory statements to ancestors) gradually vanished. Artistically derived script reached its peak with the creation of the *niao chong shu* ('bird–worm script'), and inscriptions moved from the interior to the exterior of the vessel, implying a transfer of audience from the deceased to the living.

3-SECOND SURVEY
Bronze inscriptions on ritual bronzes (mostly vessels and bells) relate chiefly to ancestor worship.

3-MINUTE EXCAVATION
As the archaeologist Lothar von Falkenhausen suggests, the bulk of Western Zhou long inscriptions comprise three parts: an initial 'announcement of merit', a central 'statement of dedication' and a final 'statement of purpose'. Of these, the dedicatory statement to the deceased ancestor, *X zuo bao zun yi* ('X made this precious, venerable sacrificial vessel'), is the most significant part. Clearly the main concern of the Western Zhou inscriptions was ancestor worship.

RELATED HISTORIES
See also
YINXU
page 34

RITUAL VESSELS & THEIR DISTRIBUTION
page 60

TOMBS OF THE SHANG ELITES
page 98

SCRIBES & HISTORY
page 130

30-SECOND TEXT
Peng Peng

As an example of ancestor worship, this lid of a bronze you vessel (top) bears the inscription: 'Earl of Hei made this precious, venerable sacrificial vessel'.

BAMBOO SLIPS

the 30-second history

Bamboo slips were one of the most important media for literacy in Bronze Age China. They were made from narrow processed strips of bamboo, and each slip carried a column of text that was written using brush and ink. The texts were usually written on only one side of the slips, although examples with text on both sides of the slip have been discovered. Different numbers of slips would be bound together with thread in a sequence, the number of slips depending on the length of the text. From the evidence of oracle bone inscriptions from the late Shang, bamboo slips might have already been in use by then. However, because bamboo is perishable, no bamboo slips from the late Shang period have yet been discovered. The earliest surviving bamboo slips from archaeological contexts date to the Warring States period. Ancient bamboo slips from tombs were discovered as early as the Jin dynasty. In around 280 CE, tons of bamboo slips were looted from the tomb of a Wei state king, who had lived in the Warring States period. The majority of bamboo slips dating to the Warring States period have been excavated from Chu tombs in today's Hubei, Hunan and southern Henan province. The particular soil conditions there allow the preservation of bamboo slips over millennia. Over the past several decades, a number of sensational discoveries of bamboo slips have been made.

RELATED HISTORIES
See also
CONFUCIANISM &
EARLY TAOISM
page 126

30-SECOND TEXT
Li Zhang

3-SECOND SURVEY
Texts written on bamboo slips provide significant evidence for the palaeography, history and literature of early China, and their discovery has enriched our knowledge of Bronze Age China tremendously.

3-MINUTE EXCAVATION
One of the most spectacular finds of bamboo slips was unearthed at Guodian, Hubei province, in 1993. This Chu tomb dates to the middle phase of the Warring States period, and the Guodian bamboo slips would have been made before the time of the burial. There were 804 strips in total, 726 of which carried inscriptions. More than 13,000 characters were written on them, all of which were in the Chu writing style.

Texts written on bamboo slips were one of the most significant forms of documentation in early China.

One of the most influential figures in Chinese Bronze Age history, Confucius' legacy endures to this day. His teachings on politics, philosophy and education continue to inspire students all around the world.

CONFUCIUS

A descendant of the Shang

nobility, Confucius was born in 551 BCE. He was a junior officer of Lu state, and became prime minister of Lu in 499. In 497 Confucius was forced to leave the state because of conflict with the Lu elites. He began a grand tour of many states with his students. Confucius elaborated his political ideas to the monarchs of more than ten states. None accepted his ideas, and those who did not agree with him had him expelled or even tried to murder him. Several times Confucius was on the point of starvation and was derided as a 'homeless cur'. He returned to Lu state after a 14-year absence, and spent the rest of his life editing the texts known as the Five Classics, until his death in 479 BCE.

Confucius advocated 'Ren' (benevolence) and 'Li' (courtesy). He called for monarchs to cherish their people and to follow moral standards in their dealings with their families and with their states. He believed that one's character should come from education and the social environment. He broke the aristocratic monopoly on education and established schools in the countryside. It is said that Confucius had taught over 3,000 students, the best of whom gained high achievements in politics, the military, literature, music and even commerce.

Confucianism was just one of the various schools of thought in Confucius' lifetime. Only 400 years after his death, Emperor Wu (r. 141–87 BCE) of the Han dynasty elevated Confucianism as the state orthodoxy. Confucius was ennobled as a duke, and schools were set up by Emperor Wu all over the country. Emperor Taizong (r. 626–49 CE) of the Tang dynasty made him a king and the mentor of all. The Confucian classics became required reading for intellectuals and the most important source for the imperial examinations. Confucius' thoughts on politics, philosophy and education have had a profound influence in China and around the world ever since. His offspring lived in Qufu, the ancient capital of Lu state, and inherited the title 'Duke Yansheng' (bloodline of the sage) for generations, receiving great respect and courtesy from the Chinese emperors.

Chao Tang & Yijie Zhuang

STONE & POTTERY INSCRIPTIONS

the 30-second history

3-SECOND SURVEY
Stone inscriptions were
relatively rare during the
Bronze Age of China, all the
discoveries of which were
on small stone artefacts.

3-MINUTE EXCAVATION
Production of metal
and proto-porcelain was
significant at Wucheng.
Inscriptions have been
found incised on ceramics
and on stone moulds
for metal production.
Although most of these
consist of single or double
glyphs, one comprises
12 characters. These were
carved around the shoulder
of a proto-porcelain jar.
Many of the Wucheng
inscriptions resemble
those found at Yinxu.

Unlike the ancient Near East, inscriptions on pottery or stones were comparatively rare during most of the Chinese Bronze Age. Unearthed stone inscriptions of this period are mainly from the Yinxu site, and date to the late Shang period. These were incised or written on stone or jade artefacts, most of which were discovered in Shang elite tombs. They are identical to those carved on oracle bones of the same period. The majority of the inscriptions specify the names of Shang elites; some record activities associated with the stone or jade artefact that the inscriptions were incised on. The longest of them consists of 12 characters, which were carved on a stone *gui* vessel. Incidental marks on pottery from the Bronze Age have been found, the majority of which consist of single glyphs. The most significant discovery of pottery inscriptions beyond the Central Plains was from the site at Wucheng in Zhangshu, Jiangxi, located to the south of the Xiao river. Wucheng was a regional centre through the Shang period. More than 120 pottery inscriptions have been unearthed here so far. Pottery inscriptions are more frequently found from the Warring States period, most of which are stamped on ceramics. The majority are names of people, places or dates of pottery manufacture, the discoveries of which shed light on the politics and economy of that period.

RELATED HISTORIES
See also
ORACLE BONE INSCRIPTIONS
page 116

30-SECOND TEXT
Li Zhang

There was a surge of inscriptions on pottery during the Warring States period, which provides invaluable information for us to probe into the history of that period.

CONFUCIANISM & EARLY TAOISM

the 30-second history

3-SECOND SURVEY
The philosophical trends
of Confucianism and
Taoism not only help in
understanding their
contemporary material
culture but also provide a
key to the polities of the
following Han period.

3-MINUTE EXCAVATION
Because of their
epistemological differences
regarding the 'Way', these
thinkers hold different
political stances. According
to Confucius and Xunzi,
governors should
vigorously try to align
themselves through
rituals. But for the Taoists,
governors should limit their
political or economic
impact upon the people.
Like the operations of
nature, governors should
simply 'reduce the size of
the state and liberate the
population' and be
minimally involved in
administrative affairs.

The generic term 'Confucianism'
refers to the philosophy of three thinkers,
Confucius, Mencius and Xunzi. All emphasized
the cultivation of virtues such as benevolence
(*ren*) in order to achieve the 'Way', or a better
life, but they suggested slightly different
approaches. For Confucius, the 'Way' relies on
benevolence, which has to be cultivated through
the practice of various 'rituals'. Mencius
conceptualized benevolence and righteousness
as 'beginnings' that human beings inherently
possess. What we need to do is to 'fill them out'
in order to become fully virtuous. Xunzi seems to
be more in line with Confucius in the sense that
benevolence has to be achieved by correcting
one's unethical predispositions and by following
rituals. Since humans have 'standards of
righteousness' they can form a society, which is a
key component in Xunzi's idea of the 'Way'. The
concept of the 'Way' is also a cornerstone in the
canon of early Taoism, but it was conceptualized
from a dramatically different perspective.
According to Laozi, the traditional founder of
Taoism, the 'Way' is somewhere in our mind, and
has little to do with practical ethics. To follow the
'Way' is to remain constant and avoid chasing
ever-shifting desires. Zhuangzi, another thinker
linked to Taoism, suggested the 'Way' is the
cultivation of complete harmony with the natural
world, but is not related to specific virtues.

RELATED HISTORIES
See also
BAMBOO SLIPS
page 120

CONFUCIUS
page 122

3-SECOND BIOGRAPHIES
CONFUCIUS
c. 551–479 BCE
Teacher and philosopher.

MENCIUS
c. 390-305 BCE
Confucian philosopher.

XUNZI
c. 312–230 BCE
Confucian philosopher.

LAOZI
c. 5th or 4th century BCE
Founder of Taoism.

ZHUANGZI
c. 365 BCE, and lived until
after 300 BCE
Taoist philosopher.

30-SECOND TEXT
Wengcheong Lam

*Laozi (top), Confucius
(right) and Mencius
(bottom), three key
ancient philosophers.*

WARRING STATE PHILOSOPHIES

the 30-second history

Known as the era of the
'hundred schools of thought and philosophy', the Warring States period witnessed a flowering of intellectual and cultural scholarship, and the emergence of major schools of Chinese philosophical thought: Confucianism, Mohism, Taoism and Legalism. There were also other branches of philosophy, such as Agriculturalism and Naturalism, which later faded away. The intellectual and cultural development of this period was not a coincidence, but a continuation of developments in language, literature and political thought and practice that stretched back hundreds of years. In the context of a turbulent period of conflict, kings of different states competed with each other to gain dominance, and advice from intellectuals was keenly sought after. Hence, in order to gain patronage from their kings, political and moral issues became of the utmost concern to philosophers as they sought to give advice on state affairs. For instance, one key aspect of Legalism teaching is the use of law by rulers in government. Shang Yang, a key figure of the Legalism school, persuaded the king of Qin state to adopt certain legal practices. A series of reforms were instituted, which laid the foundation for the ultimate victory of the Qin Empire over all the other states.

3-SECOND SURVEY
Major Chinese philosophies were formed during the Warring States period, and some of these schools of thought have had a long-lasting impact on Chinese culture.

3-MINUTE EXCAVATION
Most of the philosophical writings of the period do not survive and some of the texts we have today were compiled over many centuries. However, archaeological discoveries have yielded works that had been lost in the intervening two thousand years. In 1993, 804 bamboo slips were found in a Chu tomb at Guodian, Hubei province, dating to the middle of the Warring States period. Of the 16 pieces of writing identified, 13 were completely unknown to modern scholars.

RELATED HISTORIES
See also
BAMBOO SLIPS
page 120

CONFUCIANISM & EARLY TAOISM
page 126

3-SECOND BIOGRAPHY
SHANG YANG
4th century BCE
Politician, credited as the founder of Legalism and author of *The Book of Lord Shang*.

30-SECOND TEXT
Qin Cao

Inscribed bamboo slips found in tombs reveal philosophical writings that were long lost.

SCRIBES & HISTORY

the 30-second history

3-SECOND SURVEY
Numerous historians, public and private, have produced texts throughout Chinese history. The origin of this long-lasting tradition can be traced back to the late Shang period and matured during the Eastern Zhou period.

3-MINUTE EXCAVATION
The first Chinese chronicle is *Zuo Zhuan*, believed to have been written by the Lu state scribe Qiuming Zuo at the end of the Spring-and-Autumn period. However, modern scholars think that it was actually written later by various hands during the Warring States period. It follows the chronology of 12 dukes of Lu state, covering the years 722–468 BCE, though major historical events from elsewhere are also recorded. Its succinct style led many scholars to expend tremendous efforts to elucidate it and offer their own interpretations.

When the diviners at Yinxu made predictions and inscribed characters on to oracle bones, they were producing historical records; and by participating in divination, they were at the very centre of the Shang political domain. The powers of writing and the scribal tradition were strengthened during the Zhou period when bronze vessels became the principal bearer of written records (a tradition the Shang never adopted except for the occasional casting of their clan symbols). This practice boomed during the middle Western Zhou when the texts became much longer. They record royal or aristocratic family lineages, with common endings such as 'for ten thousand years sons' sons and grandsons' grandsons eternally treasure and use in offering'. These formalized texts must have followed models written on perishable materials such as bamboo and kept in the state archive. The scribes who kept these archives had an increasingly central role. They were important assistants to the king for events such as appointment ceremonies, feasts or legal disputes. During the political turmoil of the Eastern Zhou, they took the moral high ground, judging the behaviour of the elites with sometimes fatal consequences. There was no lack of stories about brave scribes sacrificing themselves for truth, so that the seeds of a tradition of independent historical authenticity were germinated.

RELATED HISTORIES
See also
ORACLE BONE INSCRIPTIONS
page 116

BRONZE INSCRIPTIONS
page 118

BAMBOO SLIPS
page 120

3-SECOND BIOGRAPHY
QIUMING ZUO
fl.5th century BCE
Lu state scribe and author of the first Chinese chronicle, *Zuo Zhuan*.

30-SECOND TEXT
Yijie Zhuang

Qiuming Zuo is credited as author of the first known Chinese chronicle, and thus a founder of the scribal tradition.

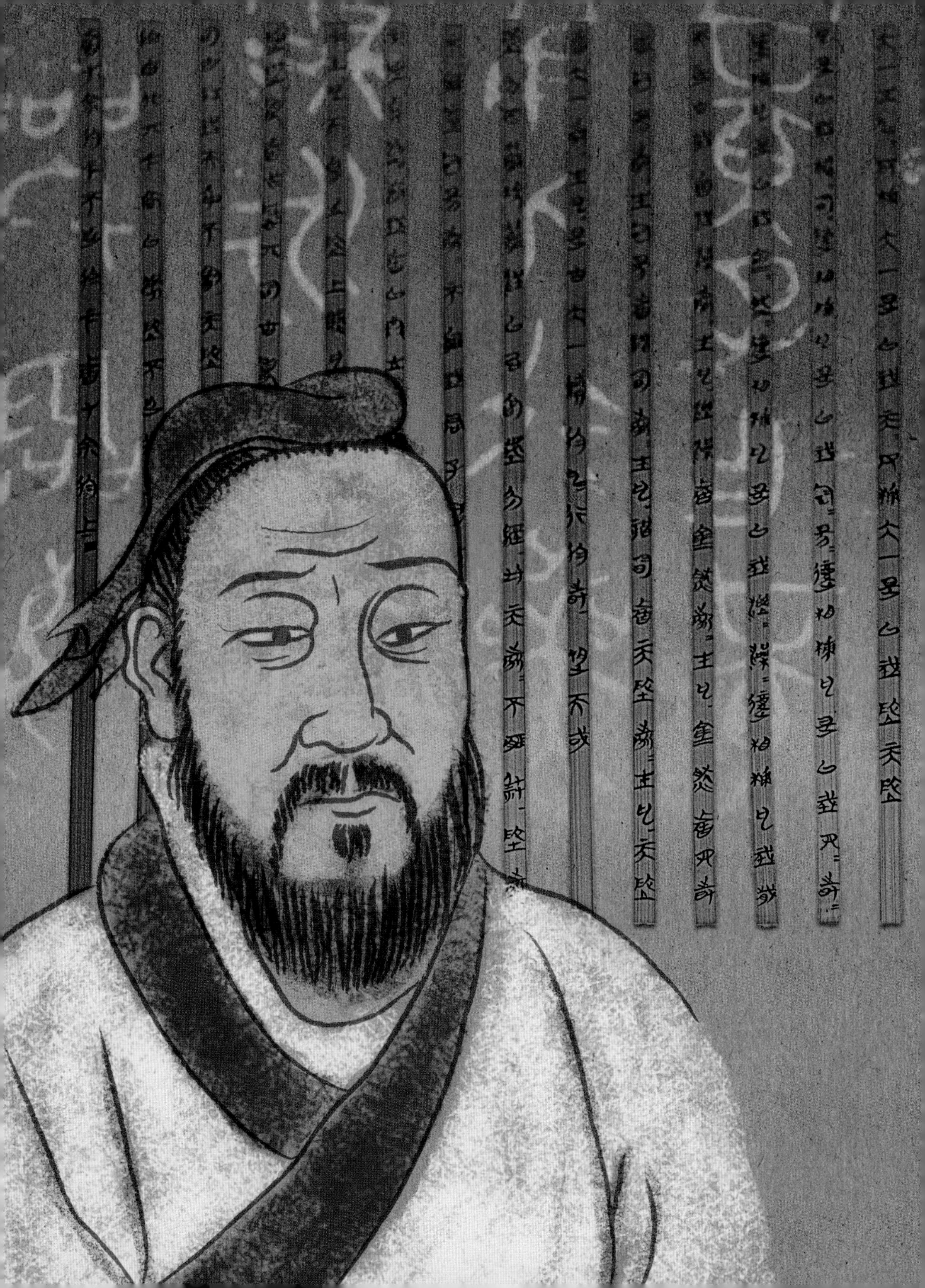

WARFARE, TRANSPORTATION & TRADE

WARFARE, TRANSPORTATION & TRADE
GLOSSARY

bloomery the earliest method of smelting iron. A bloomery is a pit or a chimney with an air supply in which iron ore is heated with charcoal. Carbon monoxide produced by the incomplete burning of the charcoal reacts with the ore in a reduction process that releases small particles of metal, which fall to the bottom of the furnace to produce a spongy mass called a bloom. This can then be worked with a hammer.

bronze an alloy of copper and either arsenic or tin, which produces a material that is harder and more durable than copper alone. Since ores of tin and copper rarely occur together, bronze working stimulated trade between different cultures in the ancient world. Bronze can be cast into various shapes or hammered into flat sheets from ingots.

Eurasian steppe an extensive area of grassland stretching from what is now Ukraine eastwards to Mongolia. During the Bronze Age the steppe supported the grazing herds of nomadic tribespeople, whose mobility was based on their domestication of the horse and probably sheep, goats and cattle. Their horsemanship was a great advantage in military terms, while the mobility of these tribes was significant in disseminating language and culture over a wide area. The Great Wall of China was built in part to protect the Central Plains from attack by the Eurasian nomads.

jade this is the name for two types of metamorphic rock, nephrite and jadeite; nephrite was the stone used for various decorative purposes in Bronze Age China. Nephrite can be a creamy-white or various shades of green, and nephrite deposits in China were mined as early as 6000 BCE.

metallurgy the science and technology of metals, including the methods of extracting metals from ores, the process of alloying, and the investigation of the composition and properties of different metals.

Silk Road a series of trading routes that connected East and West from about 200 BCE, named after the trade in Chinese silk carried out along its length, although the route also transmitted other trade goods as well as being a conduit for social, political, philosophical and cultural interchange.

vassal state a state that is subordinate to another. During the Zhou dynasty there were a number of states that recognized the authority of the Zhou court and supplied military assistance when requested. Some were little more than fortified towns, but others controlled significant amounts of territory and enjoyed a degree of autonomy.

Warring States period period following on from the Spring-and-Autumn period, 475 BCE to 221 BCE, roughly corresponding to the second part of the Eastern Zhou dynasty. As the Zhou weakened, various smaller states struggled for supremacy, and various alliances and wars took place, culminating in the victory of Qin state and the unification of China under Emperor Qinshihuang in 221 BCE.

HORSES & CHARIOTS

the 30-second history

From 1200 BCE, horses and chariots quickly became established at Yinxu. The majority of about 60 Shang horse and chariot pits discovered so far have been uncovered here. Raising horses and using chariots in hunting and fighting were of central importance for the Shang elites, and thus it was essential that these accompanied them into the afterlife. A group usually consisting of two horses and one chariot decorated with beautiful bronze fittings would be placed at the entrance to a Shang elite tomb. Horses gained a high place in the Shang linguistic hierarchy. In oracle bone inscriptions, the quantification of horses used counting words, the same as those used for humans, while other animals did not merit such distinction. The Zhou, whose ancestors probably learned the skills of horse raising and chariot driving from the tribes in the north, used horses and chariots on an impressive scale. This followed the breaking of the monopoly over the horse and chariot begun by the Shang elites, as more and more aristocrats competed for power and social status. In one sacrificial pit belonging to the tomb of a Qi state ruler, probably Jing Gong, more than 600 horses were buried, a number that the Shang kings would not have even dreamed of. Jing Gong did not have a large number of chariots, however, possibly for fear of exceeding what was merited by his status.

RELATED HISTORIES
See also
YINXU
page 34

MILITARY & WEAPONS
page 138

3-SECOND BIOGRAPHY
JING GONG
547–490 BCE
Ruler of Qi state and a major power player during the Spring-and-Autumn period.

30-SECOND TEXT
Yijie Zhuang

3-SECOND SURVEY
Introduced from central Asia, chariots and domesticated horses followed a different trajectory in terms of the development of power and social hierarchy in Bronze Age China from that experienced elsewhere.

3-MINUTE EXCAVATION
A chariot pit containing six horses and one well-preserved chariot with magnificent decorations was discovered in the centre of Luoyang City in 2002. Archaeologists were thrilled to think they had found a chariot belonging to a Zhou king. If true, as was testified by numerous historical texts, then it was possibly a final attempt by the Zhou king to maintain his ever-declining economic and political power. Soon the rule breakers from the Qin and Chu states openly used this six-horse and one-chariot pit in elite tombs.

Bronze harness pieces from a chariot team; chariots were elite status symbols from the Shang period onwards.

MILITARY & WEAPONS

the 30-second history

Warfare and violence were commonplace in Bronze Age China, and military power was essential to the political authority of the Xia, Shang and Zhou dynasties. Military campaigns featured frequently in inscriptions on oracle bones and bronzes, and armies consisting of several thousand soldiers were levied against hostile polities. The Western Zhou maintained a regular force composed of 'Six Armies of the West' and 'Eight Armies of the East.' The most common type of military force was probably infantry. Chariots were introduced by the late Shang and gained significance in both rituals and warfare. The emergence of the bronze industry contributed fundamentally to weapon production. Specialized weapons emerged, such as *ge* (dagger-axes), *mao* (spears) and *jian* (swords). Weapons were also made of jade, and most of these have been discovered in elite tombs. This symbolic representation of actual weapons in precious materials suggests the primacy of warfare and weapons. Military leadership and achievement were celebrated, as evidenced from the large numbers of weapons placed in tombs. One of the best-known military leaders was Fu Hao, a consort of King Wu Ding, who led numerous campaigns. Over 100 bronze and jade weapons were uncovered in her tomb, some of them bearing her personal name and featuring intricate designs.

3-SECOND SURVEY
Military proficiency was crucial for the maintenance of power and authority. Armies and weapons progressively became more specialized during the Chinese Bronze Age.

3-MINUTE EXCAVATION
Shang oracle bone inscriptions note that military expeditions were often led by kings and elites. Certain types of weapons, such as *yue* (battle axes), have only been found in high-status tombs, together with large numbers of other weapons and ritual vessels. It is probable that they represented an individual's military power and served as symbols of leadership. Military ability, therefore, was closely linked to identity, status and power.

RELATED HISTORIES
See also
TOMBS OF THE SHANG ELITES
page 98

THE USE OF JADE
page 110

HORSES & CHARIOTS
page 136

3-SECOND BIOGRAPHIES
WU DING
reigned c. 1250–1190 BCE
King of the Shang dynasty at Anyang.

FU HAO
died c. 1200 BCE
Royal consort of Wu Ding and a military leader.

30-SECOND TEXT
Qin Cao

The introduction of bronze technology permitted the mass manufacturing and development of bronze weapons.

VOWS & PLEDGES

the 30-second history

Even the seemingly consolidated Western Zhou regime faced constant attacks from neighbouring powers. Although he had large standing armies at his disposal, the Zhou king often had to seek help from the regional rulers. An agreement between the state and regional or private armies was established by a special event, often ending with the taking of a pledge by the participants. Bronze vessels were produced to mark such treaties. The Zhou king would not always protect the regional states, however; worse, he sometimes launched attacks on them. The regional rulers did not have the legal right to abandon their king. They could overthrow him but that would require the sanction of all the other regional rulers. Often all they could do was condemn the king as immoral, as manifested by bronze inscriptions. After the eastern migration of the Zhou court following their defeat by the Quanrong (nomads) and their allies, a period dominated by battles between the Zhou and the nomads and among the regional rulers, military alliances were essential for the consolidation of any state. At an extraordinary site in the Jin state capital, more than 5,000 fragments of jade and stone items were found in a number of pits, with characters written in red or black, alongside animal skeletons. These records dealt with the making of covenants, exchanging hostages and cursing enemies, indicating how frequently the Jin state was involved in conflicts.

3-SECOND SURVEY
At a time when warfare was the norm, vows and pledges were central activities in elite circles to expand and consolidate their territories.

3-MINUTE EXCAVATION
When the rebel forces gathered outside Yinxu, their leader, King Wu, made this pledge before his army: 'Ah! ye hereditary rulers of my friendly states; ye managers of affairs, the ministers of instruction, of war, and of public works; the many officers subordinate to them; the master of my bodyguards; the captains of thousands, and captains of hundreds; and ye, O men of Yong, Shu, Qiang, Mao, Wei, Lu, Peng and Pu; lift up your lances, join your shields, raise your spears; I have a speech to make.' (translated by James Legge from *The Book of Documents*, Chapter 30, *Mu shi*)

RELATED HISTORIES
See also
YINXU
page 34

MILITARY & WEAPONS
page 138

3-SECOND BIOGRAPHY
KING WU
died c. 1040 BCE
Son of King Wen, conquered the Shang with his joint army of different regional military groups.

30-SECOND TEXT
Yijie Zhuang

Many records of alliances have been found, indicating the importance of allies in this turbulent era.

KING MU

King Mu is undoubtedly the most legendary monarch in Chinese history. Living c. 1000 BCE, he was said to have claimed the throne at the age of 50 and to have died 55 years later. Most scholars question the authenticity of the historical record, as to live for 105 years would be highly unlikely in that era.

However, King Mu is legendary not for his age, but for his epic journeys. According to historical texts written between 800 and 200 BCE, King Mu led the imperial troops to fight against the western tribes and met the Queen Mother of the West (the goddess of eternal life in ancient Chinese myth). This meeting was recorded in a novel called *The Legend of King Mu*, the earliest novel known in China. The discovery of the novel was itself dramatic. In 281 CE, an ancient tomb in Ji county, Henan province was robbed. The robbers found many bamboo slips. Some of them were used for lighting, while the rest were left outside the tomb and were subsequently brought back to the capital for collating and interpretation.

The Legend of King Mu was among those books identified, most of which dated to the Warring States period (475–221 BCE).

The book says that King Mu had a carriage drawn by eight horses. After travelling 90,000 li (1 li = c. 500 metres) westwards, King Mu reached 'The Kingdom of the Queen Mother of the West' and held a banquet with her. This account has provoked the curiosity and imagination of readers on questions such as the route of King Mu's journey and where he met the Queen Mother of the West. Some scholars believe that he went across the southern edge of the Tarim basin, through the Pamirs, Iran and over the Caucasus mountains, and arrived in Eastern Europe. 'The Kingdom of the Queen Mother of the West' was located on the peak of Mount Elbrus in the Caucasus to the northwest of Teheran. Others think that he went to a country in central Asia from the southern Tianshan mountains. A third view holds that he set off from the Hexi corridor to Turpan, then went across the northern Tianshan mountains and reached the Yili valley.

Chao Tang & Yijie Zhuang

A painting showing King Mu of Zhou being entertained by a woman playing the guzheng. This depiction is from a period later than the Bronze Age.

THE ART OF WAR

the 30-second history

The most famous Chinese
military treatise, *The Art of War*, is attributed to
Sun Zi (or Sun Tzu), an army commander of the
Wu state. In the formation of a world made up
of a number of rival states, the practice of war
became more specialized. This period witnessed
the compilation of many texts that considered
a new subject – warfare and its relation to
states. Drawing on contemporary combat
examples, *The Art of War* is divided into 13
themed chapters, covering the key stages of
waging a war, from preparation to manoeuvring
and attacking. Many chapters are devoted to
the arts of strategy and manipulation. For
instance, the final chapter, 'Using Spies',
emphasizes the importance of knowing an
enemy's circumstances. Five types of spies –
'local', 'internal', 'converted', 'doomed' and
'surviving' – should be drawn upon to obtain
accurate information. One of the most famous
quotations from *The Art of War* is 'If you know
the enemy and know yourself, you need not fear
the result of a hundred battles'. *The Art of War*
was highly regarded by later Chinese dynasties.
From the 1960s, its wisdom was applied in
business contexts by the Japanese, and its
influence has reached beyond its original
military scope.

RELATED HISTORIES
See also
BAMBOO SLIPS
page 120

MILITARY & WEAPONS
page 138

3-SECOND SURVEY
The Art of War is considered
to be one of the classic
treatises on military
strategy and tactics.

3-MINUTE EXCAVATION
Over the centuries, many
scholars have debated the
content of *The Art of War*
and its attribution to Sun
Zi. In 1972 inscribed
bamboo slips with the text
of *The Art of War* were
unearthed in a Western
Han tomb at the foot of
Yinque Mountain, Linyi,
Shandong province, dating
back to the 2nd century
BCE. This archaeological
discovery confirmed the
authenticity of the
13-chapter treatise.

3-SECOND BIOGRAPHY
SUN ZI
c. mid 6th–
mid 5th century BCE
General of the Wu state and
author of *The Art of War*.

30-SECOND TEXT
Qin Cao

Sun Zi, author of The
Art of War, *one of the
most influential military
treatises of any period
in human history.*

LONG-DISTANCE TRADE

the 30-second history

The capital cities of Bronze Age dynasties usually served as craft-production centres which made not only everyday goods for commoners such as ceramics and bone tools, but also prestige items such as bronzes and jade artefacts that were restricted to elites or royals. The natural resources required for manufacturing high-status objects, as well as certain necessities like salt and stone, were not immediately available in the heartland of these dynasties. For this reason the grand expansions of the Erlitou and early Shang cultures are often considered a strategy to establish outposts so as to monitor the transport of resources. The best-known example is Panlongcheng, an early Shang colony in present-day Huanpi, Hubei province, which safeguarded the transport to the north of copper and tin produced from ores in the Yangtze river valley. Even though the late Shang did not follow this strategy in setting up widespread outposts, long-distance exchange continued to thrive. For example, turtle shells and cowry shells excavated at Yinxu may have been transported there from the far south, for example the Yangtze river valley or the coastal area. Scientific analysis of jade objects from the Fu Hao tomb also confirmed that considerable numbers of them are Xinjiang nephrite, indicating the existence of a trade network that linked the late Shang core with communities in the west.

3-SECOND SURVEY
The manufacture of elite goods using exotic resources and the redistribution of these items was a cornerstone of the Bronze Age political system.

3-MINUTE EXCAVATION
Long before the Silk Road was opened up, long-distance exchange between East and West Asia had already taken place and introduced not only exotic goods but also significant technologies – horses, chariots and metallurgy (both bronze and bloomery iron) – into China through the Hexi corridor before or during the Bronze Age. These exchanges had transformative social impacts that eventually became the defining features of Bronze Age China.

RELATED HISTORIES
See also
THE USE OF JADE
page 110

ORACLE BONE INSCRIPTIONS
page 116

30-SECOND TEXT
Wengcheong Lam

The discovery of jade and bronze artefacts far from the sources of the raw materials required for their production is evidence of the huge distances over which goods were traded in ancient China.

NOMADS

the 30-second history

The most common mode of subsistence for the Bronze Age nomads in northern China was hunter-gathering and pasturage, though they did settle occasionally and turn to agriculture. Scholars believe that the reason they moved southwards was the harsh environment caused by climatic changes and the consequent lack of food. In the oracle bone records, the Shang referred to the people around them as 'fang', some of these might have been nomads. A clearer picture of them emerges from the Western Zhou period. The invasion of the Western Zhou capital by the Quanrong (barbarians named *Quan*) was probably the most significant meeting of the two sides. The Zhou were defeated and forced to move their capital to the east. The Great Wall of China was also initiated, to some extent, by the necessity of repelling the nomads. Nevertheless, communication between the nomads and the agricultural communities extended beyond warfare. 'Wearing Hu dress and shooting from a horse' is an account of Wu Ling, the king of Zhao state during the Warring States period, who ordered his soldiers to learn from the nomads and to substitute short and close-fitting clothing for their flowing garments, in order to increase their combat effectiveness. The nomadic tribes also made great contributions to various areas of knowledge, such as the use of horses and chariots, metallurgy and the interchange of many kinds of plants and animals.

3-SECOND SURVEY
On the vast steppes in the north of China were communities that moved around foraging for food, some of which headed south and made contact with the settled agricultural communities.

3-MINUTE EXCAVATION
As a result of their particular environment and way of life, material remains of nomads are quite different from those of agricultural settlements. They usually lived in caves or tents, so dwelling foundations are relatively few. Ceramics are not suitable for a mobile lifestyle, so these are rarely found. Bronze tools and weapons, and gold and silver jewellery are, however, comparatively common. Animal sacrifices have also been found in tombs and animal motifs are common decorations on artefacts.

RELATED HISTORIES
See also
RIVERS & MONSOONS
page 14

HORSES & CHARIOTS
page 136

LONG-DISTANCE TRADE
page 146

NORTHERN BRONZE
COMPLEX
page 150

3-SECOND BIOGRAPHY
WU LING
Reigned 325–299 BCE
King of Zhao state during the Warring States period.

30-SECOND TEXT
Sai Ma

Animals were common subjects for gold and bronze artefacts made by the nomadic tribes of the Eurasian steppe.

NORTHERN BRONZE COMPLEX

the 30-second history

The 'northern zone' is the term used to refer to the region north of the Great Wall, where the landscape is dominated by semi-arid grassland. Because of its location, this area was a connecting route as well as cultural intermediary between the Central Plains and the Eastern Eurasian Steppe from the Neolithic period. From the late Neolithic period, this area is known for the widespread use of metal objects. Because of the generally early date of these metal finds and the region's dynamic relationship with the surrounding cultures, it is believed that early metallurgy techniques were transmitted from the Eurasian Steppe to the Central Plains via this region. However, although many cultural features were shared between the peoples of the Central Plains and those living in this region, their strategies in metallurgy were in stark contrast. Communities in the northern zone used bronze to manufacture tools and personal decorations, whereas in the Central Plains bronze was mainly used for ritual items; in the Central Plains, casting employed sophisticated piece-moulding, in contrast with the simple bi-valve moulds used in the northern zone; arsenical copper and precious metals were seldom used in the Central Plains, but were widely used in the northern zone. These distinctions indicate that this area was culturally independent from the Central Plains during most of the Bronze Age.

RELATED HISTORIES
See also
HORSES & CHARIOTS
page 136

NOMADS
page 148

30-SECOND TEXT
Siran Liu

3-SECOND SURVEY
The northern zone lies in a critical position between the Eurasian Steppe and the Central Plains of China, acting as mediator of cultural interaction between these two regions. Metallurgy was probably introduced to the Central Plains from this region.

3-MINUTE EXCAVATION
The Lower Xiajiadian culture in the Liao river valley is one of the most important Bronze Age cultures in the northern zone. It is broadly dated between the late third millennium and the late second millennium BCE. Its society was probably based on kinship, and members of rich families boast large collections of tomb artefacts, especially bronze ornaments. The most impressive cemetery revealed 60 metal objects, 52 of which were found in the tombs of wealthy families.

Tools and items of jewellery were characteristic of the metalwork of the northern tribes.

APPENDICES

RESOURCES

BOOKS

Ancient Sichuan: Treasures from a Lost Civilization
Edited by Robert Bagley
(Seattle Art Museum, 2001)

Anyang
Li Chi
(University of Washington Press, 1977)

The Archaeology of China: From the Late Paleolithic to the Early Bronze Age
Li Liu and Xingcan Chen
(Cambridge University Press, 2012)

The Archaeology of Warfare: Prehistories of Raiding and Conquest
Elizabeth Arkush and Mark Allen.
(University Press of Florida, 2006)

Art, Myth and Ritual: The Path to Political Authority in Ancient China
Kwang-chih Chang
(Harvard University Press, 1983)

The Beginning of the Use of Metals and Alloys
Edited by R. Maddin
(MIT Press, 1988)

Bureaucracy and the State in Early China
Feng Li
(Cambridge University Press, 2013)

The Cambridge History of Ancient China: From the Origins of Civilization to 221 BC
Edited by Michael Loewe and Edward L. Shaughnessy,
(Cambridge University Press, 1999)

Chinese Silks
Dieter Kuhn, James C. W. Watt, and Juanjuan Chen
(Yale University Press, 2012)

Chinese Society in the Age of Confucius (1000–250 BC): The Archaeological Evidence
Lothar von Falkenhausen
(Cotsen Institute of Archaeology, University of California, 2006)

Early China: A Social and Cultural History
Feng Li
(Cambridge University Press, 2013)

The First Writing: Script Invention as History and Process.
Edited by Stephen Houston
(Cambridge University Press, 2008)

Landscape and Power in Early China: The Crisis and the Fall of the Western Zhou 1045–771 BC
Feng Li
(Cambridge University Press, 1996)

New Perspectives on China's Past: Chinese Archaeology in the Twentieth Century.
Edited by Xiaoneng Yang
(Yale University Press with the Nelson-Atkins Museum of Art, Kansas City, 2004)

The Problem of Meaning in Early Chinese Ritual Bronzes
Edited by R. Whitfield
(Percival David Foundation of Chinese Art, School of Oriental and African Studies, University of London, 1993)

Ritual Vessels of Bronze Age China
Max Loehr
(The Asia Society, 1968)

Science and Civilisation in China Volume 5: Chemistry and Chemical Technology; Part XIII: Mining
P. J. Golas
(Cambridge University Press, 1999)

Shang Ritual Bronzes in the Arthur M. Sackler Collections
Robert Bagley
(Harvard University Press, 1987)

Sources of Shang History: The Oracle-bone Inscriptions of Bronze Age China
David Keightley
(University of California Press, 1978)

Sources of Western Zhou History: Inscribed Bronze Vessels
Edward L. Shaughnessy
(University of California Press, 1991)

Suspended Music: Chime-Bells in the Culture of Bronze Age China
Lothar von Falkenhausen
(University of California Press, 1993)

Western Zhou Ritual Bronzes from the Arthur M. Sackler Collections
Jessica Rawson
(Arthur M. Sackler Foundation, 1990)

Writing & Literacy in Early China
Edited by Feng Li and David Branner
(University of Washington Press, 2011)

NOTES ON CONTRIBUTORS

EDITOR

Yijie Zhuang is Lecturer in Chinese Archaeology at the Institute of Archaeology, University College London. He graduated from Peking University and obtained his PhD at the University of Cambridge. His research interests include geoarchaeology – long-term land use, history and landscape changes from the Neolithic to early Imperial periods in China.

CONTRIBUTORS

Qin Cao is a PhD student at the Institute of Archaeology, University of Oxford. She is the holder of an Arts and Humanities Research Council (AHRC) Collaborative Doctoral Award in association with the British Museum. Her research explores the multiple roles of weapons and their significance in Shang (c.1600–1050 BCE) and Western Zhou (c.1050–771 BCE) societies.

Beichen Chen is a DPhil candidate at the School of Archaeology, University of Oxford. His current academic interest lies in the study of China's bronze ritual vessels from the second to the first millennium BCE, including the development of casting technology, and the change of ritual performance. He is also working on China's ancient trade and exchange, especially through waterway communications.

Wengcheong Lam is a PhD candidate in the Department of Anthropology at Harvard University. His research areas include the iron technology, food system and the economic structure of the Bronze Age and Early China.

Siran Liu is a PhD student at the University College London, Institute of Archaeology. His main research interest is in reconstructing ancient metal production technologies; scrutinizing the technological choices of craftsmen under various social-economic and environmental settings; and understanding the cultural-environmental reasons underlying the technological diversification and innovation in the ancient world. He is fascinated by the inter-disciplinary nature of this research and especially enjoys a methodology combining fieldwork, lab-based scientific analysis and experimental reconstruction.

Sai Ma is an assistant professor at School of Ethnology and Sociology, Minzu University of China. Her interests lie in Chinese archaeology, especially the Bronze Age. She participated in archaeological surveys and excavations in many provinces in China. Her research focuses on social complexity, specialized production, mortuary analysis and hierarchy. Her related interests are ethnoarchaeology, modern mortuary rites and archaeobotany.

Peng Peng is a PhD candidate in the Department of Art and Archaeology, Princeton University. He has extensive experience in archaeology. He participated in excavations at Marsal (Lorraine, France), and spent nearly half a year working at the salt-producing Shuangwangcheng site in Shandong Province, China. He also took part in the Chengdu Plain Archaeological Survey Project organized by Washington University, Harvard University and Peking University. He has given presentations and published articles on a variety of topics, including Chinese bronzes, salt archaeology, origins of agriculture, archaeological methodology and Chinese local beliefs. He is also interested in ancient civilizations besides China, especially ancient Egypt, Mesopotamia, Mesoamerica and the Andean World. His current academic interest lies in the study of Chinese ancient bronzes, and comparative study of the first civilizations and writing systems.

Chao Tang majored in both History and Chinese Literature for her BA, and continued her study at Peking University for her MA in Chinese Bronze Age archaeology. She has worked at the First Historical Archives of China for several years. Her research interests include the text analysis of ancient geographic literature and how this can inform historic records and archaeological data in the study of ancient society.

Li Zhang is Assistant Professor of Archaeology at Zhengzhou University. Her research focuses on the emergence and transformation of complex societies during the Neolithic Age and the Bronze Age of China, as well as the landscape of China's participation in the Eurasian network during the Bronze Age.

INDEX

piece-mould casting 34, 56–57, 58
pledges 140–41
polygamy 90
population 18–19
pottery
    ceramics 36, 38, 44, 80, 148
    firing 74, 80
    production 80–81
    stone pottery inscriptions
        124–25
proto-porcelain 31, 32, 38, 75, 80,
    115, 124
pyromancy 96

Q
Qi Huan Gong 85
Qin Mu Gong 106–7
Qin state 9, 13, 24, 48, 108, 114, 115,
    128, 136
    cemetery 46–47
Quanrong 42, 140, 148

R
radiocarbon dating 52, 54
ramped tombs 31, 34, 98
Records of the Grand Historian 22
ritual 48, 53, 96, 104, 126
    cult 12
    reform & restructuring
        64, 70–71
    see also sacrifice
ritual vessels 60–61, 70, 96
    matching sets 64–65
rivers 14–15

S
sacrifice 34, 48, 98, 100, 108–9,
    148
sacrificial pits 24, 34, 36, 46, 97,
    98, 100, 108, 136
Sanxingdui 7, 36–37, 60
scribes 26, 130–31
shaft-pit tombs 97, 102
shamanism 104–5

shamans 97, 104
Shan family 62–63
Shang period 6, 9, 14, 18, 26, 34,
    38, 54, 56, 66, 68
    alcohol 78
    architecture 24
    calendar 88
    chariots 136, 138
    cities 22
    divination 104, 108, 116
    elite tombs 98–99, 136, 138
    inscriptions 118, 120, 124, 130
    marriage 90
    medicine 92
    pottery 80
    state cemeteries 46
    trade 146
    women 90
Shang Yang 16, 128
silk 75, 82
Silk Road 135
Sima Qian 22
skew chamber 31, 48
slag 31, 34
smelting 31, 53
Spring-and-Autumn period 13, 14,
    102, 130
Spring and Autumn Annals 13
state management 26–27
stone pottery inscriptions 124–25
Su Qin 18
Suizhou Zeng Marquis cemetery
    44–45
sumptuary laws 53, 64, 97
Sun Zi (Sun Tzu) 144

T
Taoism 115, 126–27, 128
textiles 82–83
    silk 75, 82
tombs 32, 38, 44
    burial goods 32, 60, 78, 80, 92,
        98, 100, 102, 110
    chamber 96

Chu tombs 82, 120, 128
Dayangzhou 38–39
jade objects 110
Majiayuan site 48–49
Qin tombs 46
ramped tombs 31, 34, 98
shaft-pit tombs 97, 102
Shang elite 98–99, 136, 138
skew chamber 31, 48
see also cemeteries
trade 30, 32, 146–47
tributary system 13, 16
turquoise 31, 32

V
vassal states 97, 100, 135
vows 140–41

W
warfare 138, 140, 144, 148
Warring States period 9, 13, 14, 48,
    115, 135
    bamboo slips 120
    food 76
    philosophies 128–29
    population 18
'Way', the 126
weapons 138–39
welding 30, 48, 53
Western Zhou period 8, 9, 18, 21,
    42, 54, 56, 64, 68, 70, 108
    alcohol 78
    bureaucracy 26
    inscriptions 118, 130
    jade 110
    land ownership 16
    marriage 90
    medicine 92
    military power 138, 140
    nomads 148
    Shan family 63
    state cemeteries 48, 100
    vassal states 100
    vows & pledges 140

wine vessels 70, 78
women, status of 90
Wu Ding, King 98, 104, 116, 138
Wu, King 21, 26, 140
Wu Ling, King 148

X
Xia period 6, 9, 22, 32, 78, 138
Xu Xusheng 32
Xunzi 126

Y
Yi, Marquis 58, 66, 88
Yinxu 22, 34–35, 36, 98, 116, 124,
    130, 136, 140, 146
Yong City 22, 24, 46–47

Z
Zhengzhou 22, 36, 116
Zhou dynasty 66, 88
    alcohol 78
    cities 22
    clothing 82
    military power 138
    state cemeteries 44–45,
        100–101
    vassal states 97, 135
    women 90
    see also Eastern Zhou period;
        Western Zhou period
Zhou Gong 20–21, 26, 42
Zhouyuan 42–43, 60
Zhuangbai No.1 bronze hoard 70
Zhuangzi 126
Zou Heng 32

ACKNOWLEDGEMENTS

PICTURE CREDITS
The publisher would like to thank the following individuals and organizations for their kind permission to reproduce the images in this book. Every effort has been made to acknowledge the pictures; however, we apologize if there are any unintentional omissions.

Alamy: /© Lebrecht Music and Arts Photo Library 142.
Qin Cao: 83 centre right, 139 (all background images).
Beichen Chen: 45 bottom left & right, 61 top right, bottom right & background image, 65 (all photos).
Clipart: 77 top right, 79 bottom left, 87 (hand images), 89 bottom right, 91 bottom, 105 bottom, 109 right, 127 top left, 149 bottom.
Corbis: /© Lowell Georgia: 109 left.
Ivan Hissey: 20, 39 left & right, 40, 49 centre & bottom, 106, 117 left, 131 bottom left, 145 top.
Sai Ma: 43 bottom background.
Shutterstock, Inc./www.shutterstock.com: 127 bottom right; /Alan49: 79 background image; /AridOcean: 49 top left, 151top; /Atelier_A: 27 bottom; /fotoarek: 15 bottom right; /ArtWell: 55 top; /Marilyn Barbone: 93 top; /Alena Brozova: 59 top; /changsgallery: 89 top; /Chotewang: 77 left; /Nikolay Dimitrov-ecobo: 81 background; /Fribus Ekaterina: 55 bottom; /fotohunter: 127 top right; /Lalith Herath: 129 background, left; /Jiang Hongyan: 79 top right; /Pavel Ilyukhin: 17 bottom; /Junrong: 84; /Jun Kawaguchi: 19 centre, 35 background; /Kletr: 27 bottom; /kongsky: 27 bottom; /Philip Lange: 122; / L.F: 93 background; /Tim Masters: 77 bottom right; /michal812: 27 bottom; /Jun Mu: 117 top right, centre & bottom right; /Neftali: 23 bottom; /Bill Perry: 7, 37; /TTstudio: 149 background; /Kirill Smirnov: 15 top right; /Successo images: 83 background; /Subbotina Anna: 121 left; /sunxuejun: 117 background; /EmiliaUngur: 89 top right; /Ye Choh Wah: 77 background; /Yangchao: 27 left.
Chao Tang: 81 top left, 111 top far left, 137 bottom left & right.
Thinkstock: 15 left.
Gary Lee Todd, PhD: 25 (all photos), 27 top right (both photos), 33 (all photos), 35 bottom, 43 bottom, 45 top right, 47 (all photos), 55 centre, 57 (all photos), 59 centre and bottom, 61 bottom left, 62, 67 (all photos), 71 bottom, 79 centre & bottom right, 81 top right, centre & bottom, 83 left & far right, 87 (all photos), 91 top, 93 bottom, 99 (all photos), 101 (all photos), 103 (all photos), 105 top left & right, 111 (all except top far left), 119 (all photos), 125 (all photos), 131 top & background, 137 top & bottom centre, 139 top, 141 (all photos), 145 bottom, 147 (all photos), 149 top left and right, 151 bottom left to right.
Wikipedia: 663highland: 145 main image; /Fanghong: 17 top left, 129 right; /Ismoon: 139 bottom; /Kanguole: 17 top right, 23 background; /Kenpeiu: 43 right; /Mountain: 2, 69, 71 t-op; Mlogic: 35 main image; /Rolfmueller: 19 main image; /Sharkman: 121 right & 129 left.